ALL THE THINGS I WISH I KNEW

How to Be a Fierce Chick Living Her Best Life

SARAH CENTRELLA

Skyhorse Publishing

Skyhorse Publishing books may be purchased in bulk at special discounts for sales promotion, corporate gifts, fund-raising, or educational purposes. Special editions can also be created to specifications. For details, contact the Special Sales Department, Sports Publishing, 307 West 36th Street, 11th Floor, New York, NY 10018 or info@skyhorsepublishing.com.

Skyhorse® and Skyhorse Publishing® are registered trademarks of Skyhorse Publishing, Inc.®, a Delaware corporation.

Visit our website at www.skyhorsepublishing.com.

10 9 8 7 6 5 4 3 2 1

Library of Congress Cataloging-in-Publication Data is available on file.

Cover design by David Ter-Avanesyan

ISBN: 978-1-5107-7089-8
Ebook ISBN: 978-1-5107-7090-4

Printed in the United States of America

Kanen, Mira & Izzy, being your mama is the greatest joy of my life.
Girls, this one is especially for you.
Buonanotte amore mio!

CONTENTS

PART TWO: *On Success . . .*

Level-Up Your Career*:* **Lessons to help you** *– Be the boss
babe you always wanted to be!*

PART SIX: *On Life . . .*

Lessons to help you—*Be the best you and live the best life!*

PREFACE

These pages are inspired by my clients, past and present, and particularly the women of my Coaching Circle. It has been through coaching them each week that I've learned which lessons and tools resonate universally with women from around the world, with various backgrounds, in different age groups, and across the socio-economic spectrum.

These women have taught me that we are all much more alike than we are different. That *nasty bitch* who lives in your head, saying how awful you're doing at life? She lives in all of us. Those beliefs you have about money, the ones that hold you back from your next level of success? Yep, they are buried in us all, regardless of the balance in our bank account. That fear of saying what you really think, or of standing up for yourself? It's not just you, it resides in the most confident women.

This is for Dianne, who used the coaching I share in this book to raise the bar on herself across all areas of her life in the two years she's been in Coaching Circle. Congrats on the ninety pounds lost, the finalized divorce, on hustling for the certification needed to up-level your career and expand your financial abundance. Dianne taught me how important it is for women to have tools that empower us to self-advocate (lesson #1).

This is for Melinda, who as a single mom when we began working together in 2018, used the tools shared in lesson #18 to manifest her soulmate. Congrats on your engagement, girl!

This is for Amanda, who used the tips and tools in Part Two to massively up-level her career, negotiating her highest salary ever, nearly doubling her net worth, and finding her Golden Ticket (lesson #22).

This is for Kristy, who used the tools in Part Three to substantially change her financial future, and who inspired my coaching on building wealth.

This is for Courtney, who taught me how to coach other moms using the tools that worked for me.

This is a love letter to all the women I've worked with over the past decade, who've helped me become a better coach. I learn from you each day, and together we use the tools in this book to continuously transform ourselves, and our lives, into the best possible versions of both. You hold me accountable to practice what I preach. It is your willingness to act on the coaching, to do the work, and to receive the tough love (when needed), that has helped me create tools that will impact women everywhere. We thank you.

And most importantly, this is for you, dear reader. It is all the things I've learned, most the painful way, in hopes that it helps you evolve into the fierce, powerful, incredible women you were born to be. It is the rawest expression of myself, lessons shared through the lens of my personal experience, with the hope that revealing my truth in this way might positively impact your life.

These lessons are shared without judgment and are not one-size-fits-all. There's a lot here, so resist the temptation to feel overwhelmed by that, and instead bite it off piece by piece. In most chapters I share a "coaching" section with tips and tools to help you implement the lesson into your own life. Take what serves you, dismiss what's not relevant, and just keep an open mind about the rest.

My dream is that this book resonates with you in new ways at different times in your life, and that it does more than inspire you. My loving intention is for it to provide tools that help you make desired changes and achieve new results.

Shall we begin?

PART ONE
ON BEING A WOMAN . . .

Lessons to help you – *How to be a strong, confident, fierce chick!*

These are all the lessons I've learned that I wish I knew when I was twenty. I wish it hadn't taken me another twenty-plus years to finally accept a compliment or to understand that I didn't have to listen to the *nasty bitch* in my head who's always trying to tear me down. I wish I knew my own strength *before* it was tested. I wish I knew in my thirties that worrying about other people's opinions and their judgment was simply wasting precious energy. I wish I knew I didn't have to apologize for things that needed no apology or explain myself when it wasn't necessary. I wish I knew how to love and appreciate my body starting when I was twelve years old, instead of battling with it until my mid-forties.

This section shares those lessons (and more) with the hope that you can learn them sooner, faster, and with less pain than I did. These are the things I've taught my daughters (with the exception of "get naked," that one can wait), my friends, and of course my clients.

Remember, as with all the advice in this book, it's general, and it may or may not fit you or your situation. My goal is that you take what you need and apply it to your life, so you can begin receiving the benefit of its coaching.

LESSON #1

SPEAK UP

How to self-advocate effectively to get your point across and be heard.

Does the idea of speaking up for yourself send fear and discomfort pulsing through your entire body? It does for a lot of us. I can't tell you how many times I've heard women say things like, "I'll just let it go, it's no big deal," or "It's not worth an argument." That's how they respond when I ask, "Why don't you say how you feel?"

In case no one has told you lately, your voice *matters*. Your opinion matters. Your thoughts on everything under the sun, *matter*. But you need to speak up! If you want your voice to be heard, your opinions to count, your thoughts and feelings to be considered, your boundaries to be respected, you have to tell people what you think.

Here's the raw uncomfortable truth—if you don't self-advocate (stand up for yourself, speak your mind), you can't complain when people take advantage of you, treat you unfairly, or walk all over you. It's no one else's job to stand up for you, or look out for your best interest. That's a *you thing*. And since no one is a mind reader, it's on us to set them straight, tell them what's on our mind, provide our point of view, or just share how we feel and what we're thinking.

If something seems unfair or unreasonable, say so. I know women are sometimes scared to speak up for fear of being labeled "bitchy," or a "Karen," or whatever other derogatory name is currently trending, but there's a way to be heard without being *that bitch.*

Being able to advocate for yourself is such an important part of a happy, successful, fulfilled life. It affects *everything.* If you don't speak up when someone does you wrong in business, you likely don't advocate for yourself in relationships either, or when it comes to your money, etc. The financial and emotional cost of this silence can be massive and destructive.

There are so many areas of your life where it's critical to stand up for yourself that it would be impossible to list every scenario here, but I thought it might be helpful to give a few examples with tips on what to do.

I learn from my own life, and thus my mistakes are my greatest teachers. And I've learned that when you advocate for yourself, things often turn out better than you could have ever predicted.

EXAMPLE:

In 2015, I took a job as a mortgage loan officer for a large company, while awaiting the release of my first book, *Hustle Believe Receive.* The manager who hired me said the position would be commission only. Part of this seemed normal to me because I knew commission is how you make money in mortgages, but the other part (my gut) knew that couldn't be right. I was treated like a full-time employee, with all the expectations and none of the pay. Something was definitely off. I asked my co-workers if that seemed normal and they all agreed, "it sucks, but that's just how it is." I double-checked with my boss. Everyone seemed fine with it, but me.

This is the moment I had a choice, the one we all have. I could have gone on working like all my co-workers and just sucked it up getting more frustrated every day, or I could do something about it.

I called a lawyer.

I am going to stop my story here to make sure you really get this. In 2015, I was a full-time single mom responsible for a family of four, who was waiting for my first book to be released hoping it would change my financial situation (spoiler alert, it didn't). I had no savings and was working full-time at a job that was paying me exactly zero dollars. To put it bluntly, I could not afford to hire a lawyer. But I knew that in many cases you don't need money up-front if you have a strong enough case, and so I called one anyway.

As it turns out, the lawyer took my case and I won. The money from that settlement funded a dream trip of a lifetime to Italy with my children in 2016. I never paid a penny out of pocket for my lawyer. But the part of this story that really matters to me is that because my case was successful, other employees were able to bring a class-action lawsuit which was also successful, ultimately forcing the company to stop that practice.

Most people don't stand up for themselves thinking it's going to make a larger impact. I know I didn't, but it can. All it takes is one person to fight for what's right, to change the precedent for others as well.

I share this specific example because I *know* women make a lot of false assumptions that keep them from getting what they deserve. I've told this story and had women say, "I wouldn't even think to do that because I thought, *big business always wins*. I mean, they have more money and lawyers, so why bother?" Or because, "I can't afford a lawyer." Stop assuming things! Go ask. Make the appointment. Bring the facts. Ask the questions. Don't take "no" for an answer. And for God's sake, stop passing up opportunities to get what you deserve. Speak up.

HOW TO EFFECTIVELY SELF-ADVOCATE

These tips are the key to presenting (and winning) your "case" and getting your voice heard. I learned these the hard way, from a douche-bag boss many years ago. He used to put me on the spot about everything, with the goal to humiliate me. I'd get a few sentences into answering his questions or explaining why I'd done something, and he'd cut me off. "No one is interested in the whole story, Sarah. Get to the facts. I don't care about the 'feelings,' give me the facts." Honesty, that was some of the best advice I've ever been given, even if it sucked to hear at the time.

1. **Keep it clear and simple.** Explain the situation as simply as possible; leave out the unimportant details.
2. **Watch your tone.** You know the saying: *you can catch more flies with honey?* Well, bring out the honey, girl! Ask for what you want in a tone that doesn't come across as threatening or angry. In other words, start with kindness. And yes, I get that men don't have to do this, and yes, I agree that it's bullshit, but why make it harder on ourselves?
3. **Know your facts.** When relaying (or re-relaying) the situation, keep the summary short and to the point, but full of all the important facts.
4. **Be clear on what you want.** There should be no doubt as to what you are asking the other party to do to rectify the situation.

5. **Where appropriate, ask** if there is anything you need to do to expedite the process. Is there something you can change to make things work better in the future?

6. **You always have options.** Remember that if they are unwilling to hear you out and fix it, you always have options: you can take your business elsewhere; you can walk away; you can leave a poor, but truthful review; you can get a lawyer; and/or you can share your feedback on social media. Chances are, if you are having a bad experience (with a company or service) others are too, and your honesty in speaking up can help more than just you. Anything is better than silence.

COACHING

I'm a huge believer in quickly taking what we learn and putting it into practice in our own life. That is the only way to get true value from this book. It's the difference between reading it and thinking, *aha, that's me, I should do something about that,* vs. *damn, that changed my life!* You must apply it if you want those all-important personal shifts. That's what this section is all about, and you will see it in many places throughout the book. Think of this section as your personal life coach. It's the personal work that gives you a chance to dig deep and learn more about how you operate, what makes you tick, how to tweak what needs a tune-up, totally transform what needs to change, or up-level what needs a big push.

So, grab your journal and a pen and start this discovery process with yourself right now. Answer these questions and keep writing until it's all on the page. It's the best way to see your patterns, discover what's been holding you back, and begin the process of change.

- Do I normally hold my tongue when I have something to say? Why? Do I only do this with certain people (family, partner, boss, etc.), or is it more pervasive?
- Can I think of an example recently when I wanted to say something, stand up for myself, or tell someone what I thought, but didn't? What did I *want* to say to them? Write it out. Why didn't I tell them? What did I do instead?
- Can I think of a time when a business "screwed me out of money"? Or when I was charged for something that I shouldn't have been? Did I say anything? Why not? How much money was it? How many other times has something like that happened and I didn't do anything about it? Write down a guess of how much money you've left on the table this year, in your lifetime?
- Why do I normally just "let it go"? List *all* the reasons.
- Do I feel better when I try to "let it go"? Do I resent the person eventually?
- Do I sometimes "blow up" when I don't say anything, and it keeps happening?
- Is one reason I don't speak up because I'm afraid of conflict, or of the person "being mad at me"? Where does that come from? When did that first happen in my life? Where did I get the idea that speaking up equals the other party being angry with me?
- Is one reason I don't self-advocate because I tell myself, "It's not worth it"? Or "Nothing will change anyway"? If so, I ask you . . . is your opinion/thought/point of view really worthless? Because that's what you're saying when you say, "it's not worth it." How do you know nothing will change if you haven't tried?

PRO TIP: Assuming anything is a big mistake. Don't assume people should "just know" how you feel. Don't assume people will automatically do the right thing or do right by you. Don't assume outcomes are predestined and set in stone, you don't know that unless you try. The next time you are tempted to "just let it go," ask yourself those questions, and make sure that you are not making any assumptions.

LESSON #2

YOU ARE STRONGER

How to understand your power and tap into your strength.

Do you understand how strong you are, girl? How capable you are? How brave you can be? I've gotta say, many women don't know their own strength, until it's tested. That was definitely the case for me.

I've always known I'm a pretty scrappy bitch. I mean, I was raised dirt poor and as a result have never been a stranger to hard work and "figuring it out." But I never considered myself especially "strong," or even all that capable. Until my life exploded in 2008.

At the time I was a stay-at-home mom, married to my high school sweetheart, my days spent taking care of our five-year-old son and one-year-old twins, just trying to survive. It was the recession and we'd lost our home in foreclosure less than six months prior, filed for bankruptcy, and were barely keeping the lights on, when I discovered my husband's double life. I learned of his affair through one simple text, a light blinking "unread" on his phone one evening in September while I cleared the dinner table as he showered. It read, "I can't wait 'till you're finally free, all mine, no more sharing ☺ "

Since that day, when everything I ever believed about my life burned to the ground, people have told me, "Sarah, you are so strong. Where did you get the strength to pick up the pieces and rebuild your life?" There's only one answer to this: Primal strength exists within all of us. We have it, it's there. I wasn't built with a "strong" gene that you don't have. I had no choice but to figure out a way to survive with my children, on my own. I didn't have the luxury of family to fall back on, or a savings account to help me smoothly transition out of my marriage. Instead, I had no job, no income, no savings, bills past due, and not even a car in my name. It was basically every woman's worst nightmare. And trust me, I did not feel strong. I felt helpless, alone, and very weak.

But that night, after my soon to be ex kissed our kids goodbye and tossed his wedding ring in my general direction, I realized I did have a choice. I could give up and fall off the face of the earth, or I could fight like hell to survive.

Strength comes when we stop listening to doubt. We don't get stronger by telling ourselves we *can't do it*. We get stronger by listening to that voice which lives inside each of us, the one that says, "you *can*."

You are stronger than you could ever imagine. Your power and strength are part of your genetic code, it pumps through your blood and lives in your soul—you just might not know it yet. Sometimes we don't tap into our strength until we've been thrown into the fire, but it's there all the same.

If you knew your strength, would you make different decisions? If you knew you were capable of building your life from scratch, all by yourself . . . would you? If you believed that you could make good decisions, take care of yourself, do "hard" things . . . would you take those chances and make those choices?

When we doubt our strength and our abilities, we make decisions based on fear. We marry the wrong guy because we're afraid he might be the only one to come along. We stay with said wrong guy because we're afraid we can't make it on our own. We settle for the job we don't want because we don't believe we can land or excel at the one we deserve. We put off adventure, travel, and experiences because we don't feel strong enough to do them on our own.

When we don't believe in our strength, we feel vulnerable and weak. We seek out other people or situations to make us feel "safe" and "secure," but girl, the strength you seek is within.

TIPS TO BUILD YOUR STRENGTH

Start with a motto. Mottos are one of the most powerful, effective, and fastest ways to re-train your brain, change your beliefs, and re-write your story. If you are diligent and use them often, they will work magic. I've been teaching clients how to write and use effective mottos for years and still, I'm constantly blown away at how effective they are at creating new outcomes and changing negative beliefs and behaviors.

My favorite motto is the one I used when my ex-husband left. It literally changed who I am and how I view myself as a woman. Remember how I said that I felt weak, helpless, and incapable of rebuilding my life alone? Well, every time I felt that way, I began telling myself, "I can do it, I am strong." I would say it over, and over, and over, until I felt stronger in that moment. I said it so much that before long, I began to *believe* I was strong. The stronger I felt, the more confident I became, and the more capable I was at dealing with all the new situations I found myself in as a single mom.

How to write an effective motto:

1. Identify the "thing" (fear, feeling, belief, etc.) you want to change. The clearer you are at naming the exact "thing" the better.
2. Then answer the question, what is the *new* outcome I want? Hint: it should be the opposite of your current fear or belief. This is *super* important. You must identify the outcome you *want* in order to get it.

    Example: In the example above, I felt weak and incapable. So, the motto "I can do it, I am strong," was the antidote to that feeling or belief. It created an outcome that did not exist before, one in which I was strong and capable. It did this first through words alone, then over time those words changed my belief, which changed my actions, which changed my outcomes. Get it?

The genesis of all change starts in our mind, starts with what we tell ourselves. There are endless scientific studies on how the brain can turn a lie into truth through repetition, and we normally think of this as a negative, like how pathological liars can't tell the difference between "their truth" and a lie. But we can use this same brain pathway to create new, positive outcomes for ourselves by repeatedly telling ourselves the outcomes we want, as if they were true, long before they actually are. That's why a good motto is so effective—it's convincing your brain that a new outcome is possible.

Silence the doubt. The more time and energy you give to the voice in your head that says, "you can't," the weaker you will feel. Good news alert, you can control that voice! You don't have to listen to it anymore. Start replacing it with "I am capable. I can do it." Stop looking for all the reasons why it's "too hard," and start trusting your instinctual ability to do more, be more, and achieve more than you've ever imagined possible.

Test your strength, be brave. The best way to begin understanding your strength is to do something you previously thought was impossible. And trust me, it's way better to electively test your strength than to be forced by the explosion of your entire life!

There are all kinds of ways to do this effectively. Scared of heights? Push those limits by taking a cliff hike, a hot air balloon ride, eating in a sky-view restaurant, or walking across the foot path of the tallest bridge in your city. Think you can't make it through a spin class? Take one and see. Think you could never travel alone? Take yourself out to dinner and prove you are brave, then take a solo trip to the nearest big city.

In other words, all those things you've been putting off, or have been afraid to try, or think you could never do . . . do them. You will see how truly capable and strong you are.

In 2014, I pushed myself to do my personal "impossible." My ultimate test came in the form of a terrible idea: to run the Portland Marathon. Now I want to be very clear—I am not a runner. In fact, I despise running, so this was absolutely my impossible. But after training every weekend for more than six months, I did it. It was the hardest thing I've ever done, and after running for nearly seven hours on a 90-degree day, I no longer doubted that I'm a strong-ass bitch! And yes, I get that most people finish in under three hours . . . and yes, I crossed the finish line as the clean-up crew finished breaking everything down, but hey, I proved my point, to *myself.*

We really are capable of anything, ladies.

Let your instincts kick in. I truly believe that in the core of every woman is all the strength they will ever need to get through anything. It's just part of what makes us so freakin' amazing. We are worriers, and strength is in our DNA. It's our instinct to feed our children, to take care of the ones we love, to find food and shelter if stranded on a deserted island, so start listening to it. Start acting on those instincts. Trust that when you need it, your secret power will rise up and get you through anything.

COACHING
Grab your journal and answer these questions as honestly as you can.

- Do I consider myself to be strong? If yes, why? If no, why not?
- What has made me stronger? *Write about specific experiences in your life that made you stronger.*
- Do I see being a "strong woman" as a good thing or a bad thing? Why?
- If I believed I was strong enough, I would . . . *list all the things you'd do, or decisions you'd make.*
- Have I ever made decisions because I let doubt talk me into them?
- Do I usually think: *I can do it* or, *I can't?*
- Who is the strongest woman I know? What do I admire about her?
- What's an example of something I've done that was hard, but I did it anyway?

Reminder: Your beliefs about who you are, and what you are capable of, come from what you repeatedly tell yourself. So, start saying:

I am strong.
I am capable.
I am fearless.
I am safe.
I am secure.
I am able.
I am powerful.
I am brave.
I am beautiful.
I am worthy.
I am relentless.
I can.
I will.
I am proud of myself!

Let these be the soundtrack to becoming the brave, powerful, strong woman you were born to be!

*If you'd like to know more about HOW I rebuilt my life and went from poverty to living my biggest dreams, check out my first book, *Hustle Believe Receive*, which gives my 8-step #HBRMethod for changing your life and living your dreams.

LESSON #3

BECOMING *HER*

How to become the woman you want to be.

Did you know you have a choice about who you are? You get to decide. You can be *anything* or *anyone* you want to be. No, *really*.

When I first became a single mom back in 2008, I realized that I needed to reinvent myself completely. The identity I'd created as a wife and mother was gone overnight, replaced with a cavernous emptiness. *Who was I now?* I'd never thought about it before. Because I'd been with my ex since I was sixteen, there had never been a "me," without him. I'd never known who I was outside of that relationship. So here I was, thirty-three years old, alone for the first time in my life, with three babies to raise and support.

Who was I? Who did I want to be?

I thought about these questions a lot, and slowly digested the cold truth: *the old me was gone forever.* I could never rebuild that life or regain that identity. There was just one option—I had to invent a new "me." And since I'd be composing "her" from scratch, why not create the woman I always wanted to be?

And that's exactly what I did.

It was easier for me to think of "her" in third person because she was so far removed from who I was back then, and so I thought of *her* as the "woman I am becoming."

I wanted her to be successful, so I defined what that meant and imagined how it would feel. I wanted her to embody confidence, power, and sexiness, so I thought about how she'd feel walking into a room, and how people would treat her. I needed her to be strong, respected, and capable, but also kind and empathetic. And of course, she had to be a great mom, as that was the most important thing to me. I didn't want my kids to suffer because they now had one parent raising them instead of two. I fantasized about her traveling with her kids, unafraid to give them a full, adventurous life. I daydreamed about what it would be like to be financially secure, knowing she'd created that stability independently.

The woman I am today, the life I now relish and love, is the product of my ever-evolving imagination. I *am* her. I invented this life. But I'm also *still* becoming the woman I want to be, *always.* I've learned that it's up to us to continue growing and evolving into the best version of ourselves. No one is gonna do it for us, and we sure as shit aren't gonna magically wake up as "her" without making a conscious effort to do so. It will be a deliberate choice for as long as I live.

So, who do you want to be? What kind of woman will you become? You possess the power of creation, *right now*, in your imagination.

COACHING

Grab your journal and get to know yourself a little better. Let's start creating who you want to be. Close your eyes and try to imagine "her" (your future self). This is the first step to creating who you'll become. Then answer these questions.

- How do you see yourself now?
- What would you like to change about who you are?
- What do you want to change about your life?
- What would you like to change about your personality? *For example, would you like to be outgoing instead of shy?*
- What does "she" look like? How does she carry herself?
- How do people treat her? How does she treat herself and others?
- What type of person (kind, honest, driven, etc.) is she?
- What does "success" look like on her?
- How is she as a partner, wife, mother, friend?
- What things does she enjoy?
- How does she spend her time?
- What makes her happy?

Now that you've begun to create visuals in your mind based on the above questions, I want you to write down as detailed a description as you can about *her*. Get her on paper, it's the second step to making her real!

Step three is to allow yourself to daydream about this new fantasy you've just created as often as possible. Imagine what it would be like to be her. Give her a name if you'd like, she's your new alter-ego! Ask yourself, "what would my future-self do in x situation?" Make it a thing.

Reminder: We are actively creating our identity every single day anyway, through the stories we tell ourselves and our actions, so why not do it deliberately? By completing this exercise, you've created clarity, set an intention, and identified a desire to evolve, all of which begins working immediately to manifest your new reality.

PRO TIP: Don't overthink this. There is magic in its simplicity. Don't try to go out and change all those things about yourself tomorrow, then beat yourself up when you aren't "her" overnight. Think of it as part of your life's purpose, to become the woman you were meant to be. It's an ever-evolving beautiful journey.

★If you'd like to learn more about how to manifest your dream life, check out my book *#futureboards,* which gives you all the secrets.

THE *NASTY BITCH*

How to stop that nasty voice in your head.

You know the voice I mean, right? The one that runs on auto-play in the background of your mind throughout the day, saying things like, "You're not good enough. Not smart enough." "No one will listen to you." "You're too fat, too slow, too this, too that . . ." Bla bla bla. We all have her, that nasty bitch in our head trying to keep us small, wreck our dreams, and sabotage our success.

Where would you be if you always talked nice to yourself?

It may surprise you to learn that the *nasty bitch* seems to be alive and well in all of us. In over a decade of coaching, working with literally thousands of women, she has *always* been present. Regardless of our background, our upbringing, our culture, our religious beliefs, our socioeconomic status, our country of origin, she is always present. The things she says might be a little different, her voice might sound like your parents', or a bad teacher, an old boss, a past friend, or a partner . . . but regardless, she's actively telling us a ton of BS about who we are, what we are capable of, what we believe, and what we deserve.

She's the voice that beats you up after you put yourself out there in a relationship, or ask for a promotion. She tells you all the reasons why that was a stupid thing to do and why you'll never get what you want. She's the one who says you look like a cow in those jeans, and convinces you not to buy them, or to throw them back in the closet.

She's a *nasty bitch.*

It's time for her to *go.*

The first thing I need to say about her is, she is *not real.* She is full of lies. She's a terrible mix of all the bad things we've heard about ourselves throughout our lifetime, the negative things we've thought about ourselves, cultural messaging, and our past experiences. That's her cocktail, and she's shaking that shit up and pouring us a cold glass of it every day.

Believe it or not, it's that voice in our head that is guiding our actions and getting us the same poor outcomes repeatedly. She is the voice of doubt, fear, self-pity, criticism, and self-sabotage.

SILENCE THE *NASTY BITCH*

The first step to changing the negative voices in our head, the ones who are always trying to tear us down and keep us small, is to *hear it* in the first place. Experience has taught me that these negative voices are so pervasive in most of us that they go on nearly undetected, and before we can change something, we need to know what we're workin' with.

So, what does your *nasty bitch* say? How is she putting you down throughout the day?

This can be a lot harder than it sounds, because knowing what we're thinking at any given moment, means we must be present. And trust me, being present is harder than it sounds!

SNAP IN: Here's a little tool I teach my clients to help you practice being present, so you can start noticing what your thoughts say throughout the day.

1. If you have a smart watch, set it to the "breathe" setting, to ping you hourly. When that notification pops up to "breathe," use it as a moment to snap in! Ask yourself, *What was I just thinking about? What have I been thinking about the last hour?* Take a little inventory by texting or voice-memo-ing yourself. This will help you identify your negative thoughts.
2. Set "snap in" moments throughout the day on normal routine actions. Such as brushing your teeth, washing the dishes, driving, walking the dog, working out . . . set those as reminders to ask yourself the same questions as above.

Being present takes intention and dedication; it doesn't come naturally to most of us. Think of all the times you're in yoga class pretending to meditate, but actually thinking about your to-do list. Or how when your kids or partner are trying to tell you something, you're mentally stressing over something completely unrelated. It's hard to be present. It takes training. The two tips above will really train you to become more aware and present in your daily life, helping you catch negative self-talk in its tracks.

Once you've taken inventory of those thoughts, you'll have a map to how you've created past and current outcomes. That's powerful intel. Granted, it can make you feel a bit shitty the first time you connect these dots and realize the things you've been telling yourself closely resemble your current reality. But that voice, the one trying to say you've blown it, that you should have done better, she's just a version of *nasty bitch*, so shut her down too. Because like Maya Angelou said, "When you know better, you do better." And now you know better, so moving forward, you'll do better.

COACHING

Grab your journal and list out all those negative thoughts from your above inventory exercise. Now write a list of "I am" statements that counter each of those negative thoughts.

Hint: This list should be all the things that you *want* to be, feel, believe; they are not who you are right now. They are aspirational.

Example: Negative thought: "I am not smart enough." I am statement: "I am smart and capable."

Write twenty-five positive "I am" statements and say them to yourself in the mirror every day, morning, and night for at least thirty days. I've been coaching this technique for years and it *works*. It might seem silly and too basic, but trust me it will get the job done.

PRO TIP: The most important part of "the change equation" is to *always* replace thoughts that no longer serve you, with ones that do. Enter our power mottos and "I am" statements. It's not enough to just know what the negative voice is saying; we must reverse its messaging. You must provide the new outcome.

LESSON #5

TAKE THE COMPLIMENT

Why it's important to give and receive compliments.

Why is it so hard for us to graciously accept a compliment? How many times do we deflect them instead of just saying, "thank you"?

A few years ago, I noticed this bad habit in myself, as something I'd done unconsciously, pretty much my entire life. When someone would say "Oh, I love your earrings!" I'd immediately respond, "Oh they are fake, I got them at The Rack for like twenty dollars." Or I'd get a compliment about anything—maybe it's something positive about my kids (*they were born good like that*), my looks (*that was just a good picture, I probably used Facetune*), or my coaching or writing (*I'm not a "real" writer*). I was always deflecting, putting myself down, undermining my accomplishments, and downplaying any complementary remarks.

I think I'd convinced myself that accepting a compliment meant that I agreed with the statement. That if someone told me my writing impacted their life in a positive way, and I simply said, "thank you," that would somehow make me a narcissist.

The equivalent of me walking around telling everyone, "Hey, I think I'm a great writer." I convinced myself that not accepting the compliment meant I was humble.

Then one day it dawned on me: Blocking a compliment was just another form of blocking positivity and abundance in my life. If I couldn't receive a compliment with grace, how could I receive financial abundance with grace? Blocking positivity in one area of our life is akin to blocking it in many others.

I also realized that the inability to accept a compliment was an outward manifestation of my personal insecurity. And finally, I put myself in the shoes of the compliment giver; how would it feel to have your kind words declined? Rebuffed? Nullified? You wouldn't feel heard or validated if the person you complimented constantly dismissed and diminished those words of kindness.

It might seem like a small thing, but it's not. A confident woman can graciously accept a compliment; she is able to receive kind words of praise and/or positivity.

And a confident woman can also give compliments freely. She knows that giving credit where it's due, praising for a job well done, uplifting others, building people up, and spreading kindness is a strength, not a weakness. The ability to make others feel special, noticed, seen, and loved is a unique skill, one we'd all be wise to hone.

This was something I taught my twin girls from the time they could walk. They are identical, and when they were small, they were quite the showstoppers. We'd be trying to get through Costco and constantly stopped by little old ladies telling them how cute they were. I trained them to respond, "Thank you! You look beautiful too." The smiles they'd get in response told the whole story.

COACHING

The next time someone gives you a compliment, simply say, "Thank you so much." And today, I challenge you to see if you can dish out five compliments.

LESSON #6

TRUST YOUR GUT

How to hear and trust your intuition.

If we all knew how to listen to, and trust our gut, I'd be out of a job. That's a fact. Because I believe we're all hard-wired with the world's best life coach, our intuition.

Intuition is the good voice in your head, the one you're always arguing with. It's the subtle one likely saying what you don't want to hear. But if we just learned to listen more and argue less, we'd be saved so many headaches, pain, heartbreaks, financial losses, and bad decisions.

It's that quiet voice inside telling you right from wrong, trying to encourage good choices. It's the thing sending up a parade of red flags, trying to warn us not to date Mr. Douchebag. It's the subtle voice saying, "What if you can . . ." But the problem is, we are so conditioned to hear the *nasty bitch* screaming, "What if you *can't?*" that we miss the messages our intuition is trying so hard to send.

Your gut is constantly trying to help you out, by making the hairs on the back of your neck stand up when you're in danger. Maybe it ties your stomach in knots when you're about to make a bad decision. It gives goosebumps when you're buzzing with bright ideas, and butterflies when you feel a magical connection.

I know that you understand exactly what I'm saying, because we women are famous for having a little thing called "women's intuition." It is famous for a reason, because it's always right. And when I look back on the day that changed my life forever, it was my intuition that tipped me off to check my ex's phone.

See, I was not a wife who monitored her husband's phone. I'm not a jealous person by nature, and after sixteen years together it honestly never crossed my mind that he could be capable of cheating. It just wasn't in my wheelhouse. So that's why I paid attention to the sudden, shocking, sweat-inducing thought that flashed through my body on that evening in September. Before that day there had been no signs, nothing to alert me a bomb was ticking away in our "perfect life." But that afternoon I'd watched *The Oprah Winfrey Show* while folding laundry and the topic was, *how to know if your spouse is cheating.* I vividly remember sighing to myself in annoyance. That show was the highlight of my day, and I couldn't hide my disappointment. *Why did it have to be such a boring, irrelevant topic? UHGGG.*

But my subconscious was listening when they listed the number-one sign, *if your spouse is hiding their cell phone.* It was the connectors in my brain that spliced these two things together in an instant that day while I cleared the dinner dishes, and he took a shower. In an instant the tip from the show, merged with the realization that I couldn't remember the last time I'd seen his phone, and in that same split second, *I knew.* I just knew. Knew it all. Knew what I'd find on that phone, knew who it would be, knew what it would say. Knew it was over.

That's intuition.

It had probably been trying to send me many signals before that day, but I was oblivious. I didn't know how to listen or trust it, I wasn't paying attention, so it had to eventually make shit real clear.

COACHING

I believe that our gut, or intuition, is the core of everything we are; it is our truest expression. It's the part of us that some call a soul, or the piece connected to a higher power. Whatever your beliefs, it's inside of you, and it's time we hear what it's trying to say.

1. Pay attention to your physical body. Chances are you will get the same physical responses each time your gut is trying to tell you something, negative or positive. I gave a few examples above, but can you think of any signals your intuition sends you? What are the signals for when something is "right" or good for you? What are the physical signs when it's "wrong"?

2. Look back on your life and draw a line connecting the dots of past decisions. Were any of those physical feelings or signs present for some of your biggest and best decisions? Where they there for the mistakes you've made? Getting historical data on yourself is so key to changing behaviors.

3. Find an example in your life of a time you trusted your gut. How did everything turn out in the end? Can you think of a time you knowingly ignored your intuition and did exactly what it told you not to do? How did that turn out? You see, we need proof. Our brain wants facts, it wants to know that our gut has guided us correctly in the past, so when we can see those facts in our own life, we are more likely to begin successfully acting on its guidance moving forward.

4. Act on your intuition instinct. Listen, we all know that to get a new result we must take a new action, and this is the perfect example. The only way to get tuned in to what your deeper or higher self is saying, is to start acting on its guidance. I encourage you to journal about it, write it down. This way you can go back and re-read it when you are faced with a similar situation in the future, and you'll have more confidence in your decision to act.

PRO TIP: Vetting your intuition.

In the beginning, it's hard to know what's what when it comes to these voices in our head. Which one is the "good" intuition, and which is the *nasty bitch*?

So, when it comes to decision-making, here's how I double-check myself to help decipher between the two. When I think about making one choice over the other . . .

1. Which outcome did I ask (the Universe) for?
2. Which one has components of something I want?
3. Which one makes me feel this combo: excited, scared, butterflies, and a little peaceful? That's my good decision cocktail. If it has that mix, then I know it's time to act on the guidance of my gut.

LESSON #7

GET STREET-SMART

How to wise up, protect yourself, and stay safe.

Traditional learning was very difficult for me growing up, partly because I'm dyslexic and partly because my parents didn't believe in education. As a result, I taught myself to read in my early teens and was still doing first grade math at fourteen, but that's a whole other story. I say this because I might not have been "book smart," but I have always been street-smart, and it has served me well.

Street-smarts are like commonsense "best practices," or guidelines. There's probably an infinite number of items one could list here, but I'm going to focus on the biggest ones I've used as a woman throughout my life. They are how I've kept safe and felt confident in a multitude of situations and what I've taught my daughters from a young age.

BE AWARE, ALWAYS

You should always be aware of your surroundings. Look for landmarks wherever you go, even when driving with navigation.

You should be able to find your way back without a phone if needed.

I teach my girls this, especially when we travel. I'm constantly quizzing them; did they see that sign? The store on the corner? What color was the building on the street where we turned? And I always make them lead the way back "home" (wherever we are staying). I want to know that if they had to, they could find their way back. I started teaching this awareness to all my kids when they were very young, age three or four. I pointed out the way home, I talked to them about how to learn their surroundings and how to use landmarks as navigation. That's a skill you learn as a kid growing up in the country, one I picked up at a very young age. I could help my parents navigate when I was seven or eight, and they always said that if I'd been someplace once I could find my way back. So, it seemed natural to teach those same skills to my kids, even if they were growing up in the city. These days we rely so heavily on our phones for everything, that these basic life skills don't get passed down the way they used to. What happens if your phone dies or is lost and you're in a strange city? You don't want to put yourself in a vulnerable or helpless position.

It's not about being paranoid; it's about being smart and alert. This awareness keeps you from walking down an unlit alley with your head glued to the phone. Instead, your head is up, and you are noticing who and what is around you and making smart decisions.

MAKE EYE CONTACT

I learned this from a female co-worker the first time I visited New York City alone for a work trip. "When walking alone, and a man is walking towards you on the sidewalk, make eye contact.

Don't look away." She advised. "It projects confidence, show's you're not afraid, and lets them know you've seen them. Don't look at the ground, look them in the eye." Now I know some people might disagree with this, but I firmly stand by it. I've felt confident and comfortable walking alone (day or night) with or without luggage in seedy areas from New York to Paris, Rome to Los Angeles, or any other major city. It was one of the first things I taught my girls when I took them to New York for the first time when they were six.

PROJECT CONFIDENCE

If you are alone in a new city (or even your city), don't stand around on the sidewalk looking lost. Act like you know what you're doing and where you're going, even if you don't. This is especially true when traveling abroad. If you are lost, step into the nearest store and re-set your directions or ask for help. But don't do it on the sidewalk where predators and pickpockets are looking for women who are easy targets. Walk with confidence, with assuredness, shoulders back, and head high. People can sense confidence (even if it's just projected) and are less likely to fuck with you.

THINK AHEAD

Always take a moment to think ahead when you are about to be in a new situation. This is true of a first date, an evening out with co-workers, going out in a new city, or with new friends. Just think ahead. How can you pre-avoid a compromising, uncomfortable, or unwanted situation should it arise? What needs to be in place to make sure you feel comfortable and in control of yourself? For me, it means I drive to meet people, so I can leave when ready. It also means I won't drink much, so I'll be able to trust my decisions in the moment.

KNOW YOUR LIMITS

Do you know how many drinks it takes to typically get you tipsy? Drunk? Do you know which alcohol affects you differently? This is important info that any woman who drinks should know. If you know that one tequila shot gets you shitfaced, then that's not the thing to be drinking on a first date with a person you don't know. If you know that two glasses of wine is your limit before you start getting sloppy, then only drink one when you're at a professional or work event. Know your body, know your limits, and respect both.

LESSON #8

JUST STOP!

How to stop habits that don't serve us.

STOP EXPLAINING YOURSELF

It's time to stop behaviors that do not serve us. I don't know about you, but this is a lesson I wish I had learned twenty or thirty years ago. And I'll be perfectly honest, this lesson is for me, it's a horrible habit I picked up (God knows when or where), but one that has been pervasive throughout my life. For some unknown reason, I must have subconsciously believed everyone was owed an explanation for my every action. If I was declining an invitation, I had to give this big, long explanation. If I raised prices in my business, I felt I had to justify it with an over-arching explanation. If I took a vacation, I had to explain it. Who was I explaining myself to?

Why is it that our decisions and actions need an explanation? It's true, sometimes we do need to explain ourselves (especially to a partner or someone close to us), but I'd argue that we over-explain more often than we should. This is especially true in business settings. If you are asking for a raise at work, a promotion, or negotiating anything, don't explain all the reasoning behind why you're making the ask. Just make the ask. Men don't go into long-winded explanations when asking for what they want; we don't need to either.

Do you over-explain yourself, your reasoning, and your decisions? Instead, try simply stating the decision, followed by a period. The end. It's hard at first, but it gets easier. Take a moment and think before you offer up explanations because they often weaken your position and create self-doubt in your decision-making ability.

ENOUGH APOLOGIZING ALREADY!

Ladies, it's time to stop apologizing! Reserve the word "sorry" for when it's warranted and needed. Americans have a world-wide reputation for over-using the word "sorry," and women say it far more than men. That's a lot of "sorrys"! And for what? What are you sorry for? What did you do wrong? What did you do that you regret? Because if you did nothing wrong, and don't regret anything, you shouldn't be throwing the "s" word around.

My rule of thumb is, I'll be the first to genuinely apologize from the heart when I've wronged or hurt someone, intentionally or not. As someone who's always trying to grow and better myself, I want to be called out when I've done something wrong, and I want to make it right. Sorry is about taking accountability for your words and actions and making amends.

Therefore, if none of that applies, don't say "I'm sorry." Say "excuse me," or "pardon me," but don't apologize for something that does not need an apology. It's just a bad habit that needs to be broken.

NO MORE JUDGMENT

If you're focused on bettering yourself and your own life, you'll find you no longer want or need to judge anyone else. Judging another person is negative energy and bad karma, and who wants to self-inflict all that? Not me. People who judge others are the people who don't have anything good going on in their own life, so they project negativity onto others. It's just a bad look. We don't like being judged, so don't judge anyone else.

This means stop gossiping about people. It's hard, but if you don't want people talking about you behind your back, don't do it either. I always know when I can't trust a person—if they are gossiping about other people to me (especially mutual friends), that's a huge red flag. I know for certain they will do the same about me to those friends, so I try not to engage in those conversations. It's hard sometimes, but it's just a bad look. We don't like it done to us, so stop doing it to others.

Be open, ask questions, try to understand where other people are coming from. Be empathetic, imagine yourself spending a day in their life. Can you see things from their perspective? Where appropriate, offer help or give advice. And remember the golden rule—if you don't have something nice to say, don't say it at all.

LESSON #9

WHO CARES?

Time to stop caring about what everyone else thinks.

Why do we care so much about what other people think? What is the point of all that obsessing? Wouldn't it be more productive to redirect that energy to ourselves? What do *we* think? I wish I knew long ago, that it really does not matter what other people think. Their opinions do not determine our success, happiness, self-worth, or anything else of value. It is only up to us; the sooner we learn this, the quicker we are set free.

I, like many women, spent most of my life putting too much emphasis on the opinions (silent, imagined, or otherwise) of others, constantly worried about their perception of me. *Was I good enough? Smart enough? Pretty enough?* All that changed when I hit forty. Turning forty flipped a magical switch someplace deep in my physique. Suddenly, I no longer gave a shit. Honestly, I woke up one day and could not find two fucks to give! I stopped living my life based on what others might think and started caring about my own opinions, motivations, desires, and decisions. It was one of the most liberating feelings I've ever experienced.

Since then, I've talked to many women who've experienced something similar in their forties; it's an incredible gift.

But don't worry, if you have yet to experience the lifting of this useless burden, take heart in knowing that you can teach yourself how to let go of what others think.

COACHING

Recognizing these two truths:

1. Most people are naturally narcissistic, meaning they don't go about their days obsessing over you. I know, it's shocking, but they probably aren't thinking about you at all. More likely they're obsessing about themselves, their life, or what you are thinking about them. See? It's pointless, wasted energy.
2. It is *your* life. Meaning, there should be one opinion that matters most in the world: *yours*. No one else on the planet can live your life. You get just *one*. So, the person you need to start caring about, respecting, listening to, loving, and standing up for, is *you*.

Once you embrace these two truths you begin to see the importance of focusing on *you* and not on your perception of what others may or may not be thinking. I mean, who has time for all that? If you are focused on getting what you want, bettering your life, doing things you love, you don't have the energy to waste on silly speculation. And the more you show up for yourself, the less concerned you'll be about disappointing anyone else.

If certain people in your life make you feel bad, or you're afraid they're judging you, or you're tired of being affected by their negativity . . . **get in a bubble**. I share this metaphor with my clients and Coaching Circle all the time, and it works like magic.

THE BUBBLE TECHNIQUE

Imagine you are in a giant clear plastic bubble, one that you've seen pictures of people running inside (Google "Zorbing images" for a visual). So, in this bubble you have plenty of room to stretch out and be comfortable; it is your protected, safe space. This bubble is made up of all the good things you tell yourself, all the hard work you've done to better yourself and your life; it's where your positive vibes live. It's taken a lot of work to build this happy bubble around your mind, and you're not about to let anyone deflate it.

Now imagine that every time someone said anything negative, made a passive aggressive comment, tried to label, or define you, those words stuck to the outside of your bubble. The bubble protected you from directly receiving their words and negative energy. Instead, they stick to the outside, giving you a moment of pause. In that moment, ask yourself a critical question . . . *Do I want to receive those words or not?* By receiving them, you're essentially saying, "Yep, that's true."

Now, when someone says, "You're a piece of crap," it metaphorically sticks to your bubble. You see its negativity, you pause, and you ask yourself, *Do I want to receive this? Is this true?* You have a choice; you can accept or decline it. You can now reply (or say to yourself), "No, that is not true. I know I am not a piece of crap, I am sorry you feel that way, but I do not accept that." DECLINED. And the sticky note falls off your ball and floats away.

It might sound silly, but don't knock it until you try it, because it *works*. From now on, when you are with someone who normally pushes your buttons, get in your mental bubble. Remember, you always have a choice to either receive what someone says about you or decline it. People can say and think anything they want; it only becomes true for us when we receive it as truth.

PRO TIP: No one can tell you who you are; you get to decide. No one can wreck your mood, or send you on an emotional roller-coaster, unless you let what they say in. Protect your bubble. Protect your mental health, your mind-space, your energy. Use the motto: "I control how I feel and who I am. Nothing anyone says can hurt me unless I receive it. I can choose."

LESSON #10

GET HELP

How to ask for and receive help when needed.

For a long time, I thought it was weak to ask for help. I am by nature a very independent person, and though this is something I've always been proud of, it's also held me back. I think part of me felt that if I asked for help, one of two things would happen.

1). They would think less of me, and I'd think less of myself.

2). They wouldn't help anyway, thereby letting me down and making me feel even more humiliated.

Because to me, asking for help was humiliating. I took pride in my ability to do things on my own, and feared that if I accepted help, it would discredit anything I accomplished. All these beliefs were compounded by the fact that I am a single mom, dealing with a lot of negative stereotypes about overly dependent single moms, something I've fiercely fought against. It took years of doing everything on my own, before I realized what a serious block this stubborn independence was to my overall success. The more I built my business, the more I understood I could not reach my desired level of success *alone*. I realized that if I was unwilling to ask for and receive help in small ways (someone helping me move, for example), then I was also blocking help in bigger, more significant ways, like building a team for my company.

First, I needed to address those negative underlying beliefs and change them. Asking for, and receiving help, is a sign of strength, not weakness. It means I understand my limitations and am willing to humble myself (which takes strength) to seek assistance from people I trust and respect.

Remember, help can come in many verities, including a listening ear, timely advice, mentorship, friendship, support, financial assistance, and many others.

When I realized that blocking help was a form of blocking abundance, it all clicked. I never want to be the barrier to my own success. Instead, I want that abundant energy to flow freely, but how can it if I'm willing to help others but refusing it myself? When we give but are unwilling to graciously receive, it leads to bitterness and resentment.

I will always be a fiercely independent woman and am raising my daughters to be the same; however, I want them to never fear asking for help, and never withhold help from others.

COACHING

Is asking for help hard for you too? If so, why? Grab your journal and see if you can get to the bottom of it. Where do you think that resistance comes from? How has it been holding you back? What are some examples in your own life of you doing things alone that would have been done faster or better with help?

PRO TIP: After you've journaled about it, start changing the behavior. When someone offers help in big or small ways, say "thank you." Start noticing when you'd normally block help and start making new choices.

LESSON #11

GOT MANNERS?

A little Martha Stewart goes a long way.

I am a stickler for manners and have been an avid teacher of etiquette to my children, friends, and even clients throughout my life. This probably sounds crazy coming from someone who grew up homeless and who clawed my way out of poverty as an adult, but maybe that's why I see the value of good manners. Historically in this country, "proper etiquette" was a class distinction, one of those things that called you out, for good or bad. And I never wanted to be the one who didn't know how to behave properly in any situation. If someone is gonna judge me, it's not gonna be because I don't know which fork to use.

I hated being the outsider when I was younger, so I mastered various techniques which allowed me to seamlessly assimilate with people from various backgrounds, in a multitude of social settings. Good manners is one of those things that can give you confidence in any situation. Here are a few of my "rules to live by" that each of my kids could ramble off verbatim.

NEVER SHOW UP EMPTY-HANDED

If I had a golden rule, this would be it. Never, and I do mean *never*, show up empty-handed. This means if you're invited anywhere, bring something for the host or hostess. It could be a bottle of wine, flowers, a candle, anything. It doesn't need to be expensive, but it should be thoughtful, and it should be a contribution, something the host or hostess can use right away to improve the experience of the moment. That's why flowers, wine, candles are great standby's. This rule even applies if the host said not to worry about bringing anything; you still should always bring something.

WRITE A THANK-YOU NOTE

There is no substitute for class, and a handwritten thank-you note is just plain classy. I write them after interviews, after someone has done something thoughtful, to the person who booked me for a speaking gig, after I finish working with a client, when I start working with a new client, you name it. It's a small way to show how much you value another person's thoughtfulness, business, invitation, or gift. As soon as my kids could write their names, they have been writing and sending thank-you notes for birthday and Christmas gifts and anything else that warrants a kind gesture.

RETURN THE FAVOR

A general common courtesy is that when someone does you a favor (asked for or not), that you acknowledge the favor. This means you not only say thank you, but you recognize (by telling them) that they've gone out of their way, or above and beyond in some capacity, and that you genuinely appreciate it. I am a big believer that things should be mutual; I should not ask for something I am not willing to give myself. If you are going to accept a favor, do it with graciousness and make sure the giver knows you will gladly repay it at any time.

OFFER A HAND

Chivalry is not dead, nor should it be. Open a door for the woman carrying a kid on one hip and a grocery bag on the other. If you see an elderly person struggling, be the person who offers to help. And *always* pitch in to clean up when you are at someone's home. Don't wait for them to ask, don't watch them do all the dishes from the dinner party, don't ask if they need help (because they will normally decline)—just pitch in. Start helping.

When my kids were small we had a rule that they would never go to someone's house without cleaning up all the toys before we left. This was a non-negotiable and as such they never complained, they just knew that if I said we'd be leaving in a few minutes, it was time to start cleaning. I taught them to always leave a place better off than when you found it. So even if there were toys all over the playroom when we arrived and the other mom said, "don't worry about it," my kids and I would take ten minutes and leave the room clean. This is also a metaphor for how to show up in life—leave places better than you found them, be a blessing.

LOOK PEOPLE IN THE EYE

This is something I've drilled into my kids, even though my daughter Mira is a little resistant, so I get that this might not come naturally to everyone. But it's important. If you are not making eye contact, or looking at the person who's talking to you, it's disrespectful. We need validation that what we say is being heard, and eye contact is a great silent communicator.

49

Direct eye contact also conveys confidence, self-assuredness, and can appear fearless even when we are afraid. It's a powerful tool, so use it to your advantage.

CARRY CASH FOR THE TIP

My son was probably seven or eight when I started giving him the money to tip the valet, or the person carrying our luggage at the hotel. I explained to him how tips worked and that he should always carry cash. After all, you don't want to be that ass-hole who says, "Sorry I don't have any cash." Nope, be prepared, respect the people who depend on tips, and don't stiff them because you aren't prepared or didn't think ahead. You should always have $5, $10, and $20 bills in your wallet or purse tucked away somewhere. When my son went off to college, my teen daughters took over his job as the designated tippers. They know how much to tip for their hair, nails, pedicures, and a meal at a restaurant. There is no excuse for not leaving an appropriate tip.

KNOW HOW TO SET AND EAT AT A FORMAL TABLE

Again, I might be a weirdo here, but it was important to me that all my kids knew how to properly eat from a formally set table. I never wanted them to feel out of place or uncomfort-able either out to eat at a fancy restaurant, or invited to an upscale dinner, so I taught them. I think every woman should know which fork goes with which course, where the wine glass goes when setting a formal table, which wine glass to use for red and which to use for white. If the idea of setting a for-mal table or attending a formal dinner gives you hives, watch a YouTube video or read a blog about it. It's not hard to pick up, but it is one of those things that either makes you feel at ease, or brings anxiety.

KNOW HOW TO COOK A MEAL

This might sound old-fashioned, but I think everyone should know how to cook a good meal for themselves and the ones they love. This is something I taught all my kids. You don't have to become a chef, but you should have at least one dish that you've perfected, something that every time you make it, people are amazed! If you follow me on Instagram (@sarahcentrella) you'll see that I'm constantly cooking, but nothing I make is complicated. It's all simple, but delicious.

Cooking is one of those things that you get better at over time, and the better you get the more fun it is. I use Pinterest for all my recipes and meal inspiration. They are good, easy to follow, and most are quite simple. One of my "wow factor" dishes is so easy to make it's almost embarrassing. It's cajun salmon with a mango pineapple salsa, served with rice pilaf and a garden salad. It takes about fifteen minutes to prepare, you can find the recipe for it (or something similar) on Pinterest, and it is foolproof.

- Rub salmon with spices, bake for 12 minutes.
- Make delicious salsa with fresh ingredients (a fun task for kitchen helpers to do)
- Grab a box of organic rice pilaf, throw in a pot.
- Toss some organic baby greens in Newman's Balsamic dressing, add some goat cheese and candied nuts on top of the salad, and presto!

Fifteen minutes later, you have a meal that would cost you $40 a plate at a restaurant.

So, find something you love to eat, invite your girlfriends over, and try a few recipes. Let them be the judge of the best one, and there you go. Next time you have a hot date, want to make something special for your family, or yourself, you'll know exactly what to prepare.

DON'T ORDER MORE THAN YOUR HOST

I learned this lesson the hard way, from my Grandma Noni. I was twenty-two years old, living with her at the time, and let's be honest, I had a lot to learn about everything. One night my aunt took Noni and me out to a fancy dinner. It was clear she would be picking up the check as the dinner was her treat, so I settled in for a good time. She ordered a martini, so I did the same. She passed on ordering an appetizer, but I wanted one, so went ahead with my order. The waiter asked if I wanted a second martini, and while my aunt still sucked on her first, I said I'd love one. Dinner came, I ordered wine . . . okay you get the idea, I made an ass out of myself. But the sad part is that I had no idea I'd broken some basic etiquette rules.

Noni set me straight as soon as we got home. "You can't order more than your host, Sarah." She said. "It's rude. You wait for her to order another drink, then you can order another one. If she doesn't get an appetizer, you don't get one either, unless she made it clear to order anything you want, which she didn't." I'll tell you what, I've never made that faux pas again!

So, the moral here is that when you know the host is "treating you" to dinner, follow their lead.

COACHING

Manners are one of those things that are often passed down in families from generation to generation. Maybe ask your mom or grandma what some of their "golden rule" etiquette manners are. It's a great way to learn more about your own history and pass those on to friends or your own children.

LESSON #12

WOMEN ARE YOUR FRIENDS

How to embrace and connect with women.

When I was growing up, women were foes, not friends, and there seemed to always be this weird competitive energy between females. Instead of being supportive and uplifting, we often backstabbed and betrayed each other. A strong woman would size up another chick and see a threat that needed to be handled. Now, I'm not proud of this, I'm just sayin' this was the culture of the 1990s and early 2000s, and probably long before that.

Thanks in large part to the #MeToo movement, this dynamic has begun to rapidly shift, connecting women in a meaningful, positive way. It showed us how powerful we are together, how much more we can accomplish when we are allies and not enemies. It revealed our comparable experiences and highlighted our similarities over our differences. I am indebted to the women of our generation for starting this revolution and am immensely grateful my daughters will come of age in a world of empowered women.

But the lesson I wish I knew twenty years ago, is that having a tribe of badass women in your corner makes you unstoppable.

When women are unified in their support of one another it is intensely powerful, and we all benefit.

I remember back when I wrote my first book *Hustle Believe Receive* in 2015, people asked, "Is this book for women?" It was not, I was adamant about this. And when asked, "Why don't you do events specifically for women?" I remained defiantly resistant. I didn't want to be pigeon-holed as a women's-only coach.

Here's the honest truth—growing up, I was one of those chicks who related better to men. I never particularly felt liked or welcomed by women and could name my female friends on a few fingers. God, I was bull-headed and stubborn. I can see that now. It took time before I began letting my guard down, started opening up, and allowed the real me to connect with women. I wish I listened sooner.

Today, I am surrounded by a beautiful sisterhood of clients, friends, and mentors who continuously impact my life in a powerful way. I had to embrace women and my connection to them, before my career really began taking off. It's led to two books and a successful coaching practice exclusively for women, which includes international retreats. I found my best, happiest self when I learned how to build these soulful connections.

COACHING

So, how do you genuinely connect with women you admire? Be vulnerable, authentic, honest, real, and loyal. You work to gain and keep trust. Being vulnerable and owning who I am was the catalyst to building powerful relationships with women I admire. Sometimes you need to be the one to initiate the friendship, and initially it will take some effort and consistency, as with any relationship, but good friendships with amazing women are worth every bit of effort.

PRO TIP: Always bring value. Be the person who offers, not the one who always asks. Be the one who gives, not the one who always gets. Bring something to the relationship and know what that is. It could be loyalty, a listening ear, honesty, but whatever it is, know that you are always bringing something to the relationships you are in and expect the same in return.

LESSON #13

BUY YOURSELF FLOWERS

Don't wait, treat yourself!

The other day I was at Trader Joe's picking up my weekly haul of fresh flowers and as I approached the cashier to check out, her face lit up with animated joy. "Wow! These are so beautiful, who are they for and what's the occasion?" I smiled and replied, "They are for me, and I'm the occasion." She laughed. "Oh, I just love that," she said, scanning each one and carefully loading them back in the cart. "Don't ever wait for anyone to buy you flowers, treat yourself," I told her, after she explained how she'd never thought of buying flowers for herself.

Fresh flowers are one of my passions and something that brings me great joy, and for most of my life, I thought it was someone else's job to buy them for me. But it's not.

Flowers are not an extravagance; they are a necessity! Every woman should feel free to treat herself the way she wants to be treated and get her own bouquets. Even when I was on a very limited income, I've always had fresh flowers in the house. They are a small way to show love, bring happiness, and add a warm, homey vibe.

Here are five tips for arranging store-bought flowers that look like ones made by an upscale florist:

1. **Get new vases**. My guess is that the ones under your sink are not it! They should be short and fat, no more than 5 to 6 inches high with a wide mouth. You don't buy flowers so you can see the stems, you want the petals to be the attention grabber, and lower is better.

2. **Choosing your flowers:** If the pre-mixed bouquets look okay, you can jazz them up by grabbing an additional bunch of a single flower that is already in the bouquet. This way you can remove some of the greenery and add in more flowers. Also, monochromatic colors are always a great choice, all white with a little greenery is my go-to. My favorite supermarket flowers are tulips, roses (white or pink), hydrangeas, and something wispy.

3. **Cut the stems.** Just because flowers are sold on long stems does not mean they should ever be put into a vase that way. Take two to three stems at a time and cut them nearly in half, enough so they will only be six inches or so above the top of the vase. Once they are all cut and in the vase, start arranging each flower and cutting the stem as needed so that there is height in the center, and it decreases from there. Height and variation is important. Then cut some shorter to show just above the vase rim; this gives fullness and presentation-style marks from any vantage.

4. **No leaves in the water.** Cut off all leaves from the stems so there are none in the water. The leaves are what makes the water brown and the stems rot.

5. **Change the water every three days.** I like to just tilt out the old water from the side of the vase and then refill from the sink faucet; that way it doesn't mess up the

arrangement by removing and replacing the flowers. They should last you a week.

COACHING

Grab a bunch of tulips or hydrangeas each week at the supermarket, play around with arranging them, and take fresh flowers as a hostess gift the next time you swing by a friend's house. There is just something universally wonderful about keeping and giving fresh flowers. Don't wait for anyone to give them to you—give them to yourself!

PRO TIP: Flowers don't need to be spendy. I love getting mine at Trader Joe's, because they are so inexpensive and they offer a great variety of interesting choices. I can easily make four or five beautiful bouquets for the entire house on about $40 a week!

THE #SelfPrideChallenge

How to take pride in your body, health, and appearance.

I have struggled with my weight and body image since the time I was twelve years old. I remember being at a friend's house, standing on the digital scale in her bathroom, and seeing 145 in red on the little back reader screen. It's doubtful I had any concept of what those numbers meant, but instinctively I knew they represented something shameful. I didn't dare tell my friend what the scale said, because I knew her number was much lower than mine. She was "good," and I was "bad."

Was it social conditioning? Societal pressure? Nope. It was something instinctive in me, almost primal. That's what was so grotesquely sick about my young obsession with my body and weight, because it wasn't influenced by society or the media. I grew up off the grid, one of six children, to parents who believed the end of the world was imminent, and that exposure to anything mainstream would send us directly to hell. At twelve I had never seen a magazine, watched TV, listened to secular music, or seen photos of anorexic models. Not only that, but I was raised an organic vegan; we ate only unprocessed food and grew most of what we ate, so it was healthy eating before there was such a thing. Yet still I knew I was considered "chunky," and that being "fat" made me *less than* my friends who were naturally thin. Isn't it ridiculous how we come up with these ugly internal stories? The saddest part is they become our belief systems, creating self-fulfilling prophesies throughout our life.

I share this because I bet I'm not the only one who carried insanely unhealthy thoughts about body image into adulthood. Maybe you can relate?

Because of all those negative self-thoughts, I found as an adult that no matter what diet or exercise program I tried, nothing ever worked. I could kill it at the gym, starve myself, or only eat fat, or not touch a starch, but it didn't matter, nothing changed. So, I gave up entirely for a few years, just said, *fuck it! Why bother?* If I could eat a pint of ice cream while binging *Real Housewives* and remain the exact same weight as when I'm psychotically working out and obsessing over what I eat, then *why the fuck wouldn't I just eat ice cream?*

Three years passed like this, and as I'm sure you've guessed, I felt exponentially worse each year. The number on the scale had barely increased (yes, it's shocking) in all that time, but my body stopped functioning like the body I recognized. I was tired all the time, couldn't think straight to save my life, felt squishy all over, started hiding in the back of photos, stopped showing up for my business, stopped doing fun things with my kids, and couldn't walk up three stairs while holding a conversation. I was a mess.

One day in July 2019 I was relaxing in the sun on my back patio and caught a glimpse of myself in the sliding glass door. I was shocked. It was the first time I saw what I was doing to myself, and it was not cool. *Where is your self-pride, girl?*

I thought. I snapped a picture of myself in that reflection and it's still in my camera roll (under favorites) to this day, because I never want to forget what I looked like and how I felt when I let pride in myself go.

I began by changing the one piece of the equation I'd never tried before, my thoughts and beliefs. I created the #SelfPrideChallenge (www.selfpridechallenge.com), a free mental and physical reboot, so my followers could join me in getting our mind and bodies in sync. Listen, I know the power of mindset, and the creative energy our thoughts hold; it's been the cornerstone to my own transformation and success, but I'd never quite applied it in this specific way before. This is *all* I did; you can do it too.

1. I committed to move my body for twenty minutes a day. That's it. Not a workout class, not a run, not two hours of cardio, just stand up and move.
2. I committed to using daily mottos which spoke into existence the outcomes I wanted, built me up, and ultimately would change my negative beliefs.
3. I committed to drinking eight glasses of water a day.

That's it. It was so much easier than any diet or exercise plan I'd ever tried, that I was finally able to fully commit. My expectations were not that I'd lose a ton of weight and solve how I felt about my body overnight, but that I'd begin to feel physically and mentally *better*. I knew I could do twenty minutes a day for thirty days; it was manageable. And each day I kept my promise to myself, rising to the challenge, and loved the positive feeling of daily accomplishment. My confidence slowly began to build, my energy rejuvenated, my mind cleared up, the mottos gave me hope, strength, and power. And at the end of thirty days, I had shockingly lost nine pounds, the first weight I had lost in nearly a decade.

I've kept those promises to myself ever since. I take a Barre3 class five days a week, drink my water, take my vitamins, and use my positive mottos and I've lost a few more pounds and gained a ton of self-pride and confidence. Today I can say (and mean it) that I love my body, love its many flaws, love that it responds when I consistently take care of it, love that it is healthy, love that it looks good and that I feel good in it. I so wish I had learned this lesson when I was younger, it would have saved me so much pointless self-hatred.

The good news is that my teenage daughters are growing up in a much different environment. I've taught them from birth to only talk nice to themselves, so they've grown up with the three of us saying things like "I feel beautiful today!" We give each other compliments constantly, and if one of us slips up and says something negative about how we look, the other will call you out instinctively. "Hey! We don't say that in this house!" they will hear me yell down the hall, followed by the universal reminder of, "Only say kind and loving things, thank you!" I'm not going to pretend they will grow up without body image issues or even that they don't feel some of that now, but I am proud that we have changed the conversation and shifted the value in our home to who they are, not their weight.

COACHING

Go sign up for my #SelfPrideChallenge, and you'll get the mottos each morning in your email that are created to help you build confidence, encourage you to move your body, and help change the negative beliefs about what you're capable of. It is truly an empowerment challenge, and women from around the world have done it with amazing results, many doing so multiple times. It's incredible the connection our thoughts and beliefs have with our physical body; they drive our outcomes and if they're out of sync we won't achieve desired results.

PRO TIP #1: Find an exercise that you enjoy, and do it consistently, but set realistic goals you know are achievable. Your body needs to be taken care of; it will work so much better, if you give it this respect. Moving your body consistently will clear your mind, help new ideas form, give you inspiration, and makes you feel like a sexy bitch, so make it a priority! And vow to never let it be an option again. It's not something you gotta talk yourself in and out of, it just is something you do, for *you*.

PRO TIP #2: Put it in your schedule. Nothing happens these days if it's not in my calendar. That's why I sign up for my Barre classes two weeks in advance, that way nothing gets booked over them. Also, I make sure the class is at the same time every morning, so it becomes a no-brainer habit. Just something I do almost on autopilot. SCHEDULE IT.

LESSON #15

THE REAL ON AGING

A letter to my daughters and all young women.

My Darling Daughters,

Right now, you are teenagers, and your skin is porcelain, smooth, and glowing. In summer, it turns this fantastic shade of deep golden brown, when it's been kissed by the sun (even when I've coated it in layers of SPF 50). Your hair is ten gorgeous shades of blond, from bright white to soft brown, resulting in natural highlights most women would kill for. Your eyebrows are thick and overgrown, your eyes clear and bright.

You are truly perfect.

So, I thought I'd let you know what's looming in your future, say in about thirty years. Now this isn't to depress you, or scare you, it's just all the things I wish someone had told me when I hit my forties. Sure, I'd heard "it's all downhill once you hit forty." But no one ever expanded on what exactly would be sliding down that hill. And besides, I was like you, I always believed that it would never happen to me. I'd be the one exception in history that would never be damaged by age. Yes, I know you think that too, and you'll keep thinking it through your thirties, as you should. But then one day you might wake up and say, "Hold the fuck on . . . wasn't my eyebrow *above* my eyelid?"

And this is why I'm gonna give you a heads up, that way there will be no surprises. Also, because by the time you hit forty, I will be like, seventy-something, and won't remember shit. All of this will seem like the *good old days*, and I'll probably say something stupid like, "Oh, don't worry about it honey, it's no big deal." I'll say that because at seventy, saggy eyelids will be no big deal. But it is a big deal. It's a seriously *huge* deal. There's nothing like feeling and looking twenty-something, all the way up to forty, then waking up and not recognizing the face in the mirror.

I'm not going to minimize it. It's terrifying. It's like, you've known all your life who you are, you've taken more selfies than any human should be allowed to take, you know your face. You even love your face. But suddenly you stop taking selfies. Then you stop getting in your friends' selfies, then you don't let anyone post a picture of you until you approve it, then you start using filters, then you stop taking pictures. . . . It's all bad.

Here's the truth about all this madness: It's not narcissism. It's not denial. It's not because you want to misrepresent yourself or lie to the world . . . it's because you don't believe that it's real. Maybe it's just a bad day. *Maybe your face is just puffy because you had too much wine last night. Maybe those wrinkles on the side of your face, streaming from your eyes, are because you slept on your pillow wrong. Maybe your disappearing jaw line is just because you've put on a few pounds and they all showed up under your chin, or where your chin used to be.*

It's not that we want to look younger or be younger. It's that we want to still look like *ourselves*. I want to look in the mirror and know who's looking back. I want to recognize her and love her the way I always have. But it seems like every day she's morphing into something I've never seen before. Someone I don't know. I feel the same inside, so why is everything on the outside changing so fast?

Before I hit forty, I thought those Hollywood-type women, the ones who did all this crazy shit to their face, were just in denial. Now I get it, maybe not to that extreme, but I understand the desire to just keep looking like, *me*. I don't want to walk around with some stranger's face. I want mine.

I want eyes that don't have to be propped up by Botox every five months. I want lips that are full, not injected. I want to make a kiss face without old-lady lines above my upper lip. I don't want to find a new brown spot the size of my pinky nail on my face every other month. I want to get out of bed in the morning and put my pants on standing up, not sitting down because it's nearly impossible for my legs to raise that high first thing in the morning. I want to make it through the whole day without dying for a nap. I want my back to stop hurting, my head to be clear, my eyes not to blur when I try to read something with normal typeface. I want boobs that don't flop like bouncy balls once I take off my bra. I want to work out and see results. I'm tired of plucking chin hair and getting my lip waxed. And pulling out stray gray hairs.

I'm not in denial, I just *can't fucking believe this is real life right now!* That's not technically denial, right? Aging is hard, my darlings. I wish someone had explained all this to me so I wouldn't always feel like I'm losing my mind. I wish I knew the difference between what's normal, and what makes me want to spend hours on WebMD wondering if I'm dying.

Sometimes I study my face in the mirror trying to get to know this woman. Trying to become friends with her, looking for someone I know. I try to imagine what I'll look like at fifty, and yes even at seventy. I can't imagine it. I touch my cheek bones and wonder if my skin will sink in around them, or simply go sledding down my neck. I wonder if my eyes will be so heavy and wrinkled that it will make it hard for them to stay open. I wonder if I'll still see me when I look in my eyes. That's the one thing that won't change, right? But even my eyes are changing, they get glassy, and aren't clear the way they were just a few years ago.

What then, will remain?

Well girls, you know what won't change? Our spirit, our grace, our fight, our love, our soul. That is going to be there with me through each decade, as it will for you. So, when we don't recognize the outside, we'll always know who we really are. That's how I've raised you, to love your mind, your heart, your spirit, and your personality. Those things will always remain, even when your beautiful skin begins to spot, or sag. You will still always be you under it all. Just as you'll watch me morph into this new version of me, one that I hope won't ever change under the wrinkles, the extra pounds, and the eventual gray hair.

Love,
Mamma

LESSON #16

SELF-CARE

How to make taking care of you a lifelong habit.

We hear a lot about "self-care" these days and it seems to mean a million different things, so I am just going to share my version with you. I'll focus here on the physical care, but I haven't forgotten about the mental and wellbeing aspect, which will come in later chapters.

GET DRESSED

First, ladies, get dressed! I know Lululemon made it cool to run around all day in "workout" clothes giving off the impression of our daylong athletic conquests, but let's get real, they are just an upgrade on sweats. And sweats are a tiny upgrade from pajamas. And I hope you don't leave the house in pajamas every day—though I know many of us did during COVID in 2020, but that's a different story.

I know you may not be guilty of this, but someone reading is. Get dressed (at least five days a week) in real clothes. If you don't have anything you like, that fits well, go buy a new outfit, one that can be used with various pieces in your wardrobe. You don't need to break the bank; go to Nordstrom Rack or T. J. Maxx and find something that makes you feel great.

BRING OUT THE LIPSTICK & HEELS

Dab on a little lipstick, throw on some heels, fix your hair, do your makeup. In other words, take care of yourself. Your appearance matters. That might sound a little 1950s, but guess what? It's true. It does matter how you look; you are judged for it all day, every day, whether you know it or not. When we take the time and effort to put ourselves together, it makes *us* feel better, so do it for yourself, and by extension you'll be prepared when you run into a client, or a PTA mom at the grocery store, or meet that hot guy in line at Starbucks. It's part of preparing yourself for a successful day. It's a small thing that will help you feel more organized, better prepared, will raise your confidence, and will help keep up your positive energy.

TAKE CARE OF YOUR SKIN

Botox isn't gonna solve all your skin problems like a magic eraser, so take care of it now. I can't tell you how many women I've known who did not have a daily skincare routine, or even regularly apply face moisturizer. We only get one face, ladies, so we need to take care of it.

Find a skincare line that works well for your skin type, one that includes a face wash, day moisturizer (with SPF 45), night moisturizer, and an eye cream. You can always add in a serum or a toner, but those are the basics. Personally, I've used Origins since I was eighteen and it's what I have my girls using as well. One reason is because it's organic, and I try to limit the chemicals pouring into my body. I'd rather save those for Botox. The other is simply that it has worked for me.

USE SUNSCREEN

Ok, so yes, I *love* the sun. I've been worshiping it since I was a teenager lathering my skin with baby oil and baking for entire afternoons. But I'm not a fan of the age spots it's planted on my face, so I wear sunscreen. Keep that skin looking young and lower your risk of skin cancer; it's a no-brainer.

DRINK YOUR WATER

Part of my #SelfPrideChallenge is drinking eight glasses of water a day, primarily because I'd only been drinking one or two. As soon as I upped my water intake, the puffiness in my face went down, my bloating went away, and I think it's helped me lose weight as well. I know I wasn't drinking enough water before, and it caused prolonged headaches and indigestion, acid reflux, and a bunch of other nasty symptoms. As soon as I began properly hydrating myself, all that went away. Plus, it gives your hair and skin a beautiful glow, so get that water count up.

TAKE YOUR VITAMINS

You know the benefits of this, and I bet there are bottles of vitamins in your cabinet, so take them. Every day. That's all.

ONE HUNDRED STROKES

My mother always said that a lady should brush her hair 100 strokes every night, and it was good advice. My hair has been my most identifiable physical trait all my life, something I've taken pride in, and daily brushing is one of the reasons it remains healthy and shiny to this day.

GET A FACIAL & MASSAGE

I used to think spa treatments were luxuries for the rich; now I know they are a perfect way to treat myself for any reason. I am happy to skip my latte, if that means I can get a facial once a month. And every woman should have a few massages a year; our body needs those muscles released and relaxed. We deserve it!

GET NAKED

This might seem shocking to say, but you should definitely take some nude pictures. After I ran a marathon when I turned forty, I took a bunch, they were just for me and are locked away in a vault but I'm glad I have them. They made me feel proud and sexy and I will never be that young again, so why not?

My only warning is to be careful who you send them to. These days things can hit the internet and never come back, so be smart about it. My mom always said, "Don't do anything you don't want to see on the front page of a newspaper." So, that's what I ask myself: Will I be okay if this gets out? And honestly, I looked good as shit back then, so yeah, I'll happily own them!

GET PROFESSIONAL PHOTOS

If you haven't ever had a professional photoshoot, it's time to book one. Ask your friends or a local Facebook business or moms' group for a recommendation and get your hair and make-up done before the shoot. Bring several outfit changes and pick a versatile location. There should be some good professional shots, ones you can use for work bios and LinkedIn, but also do some fun ones where you feel sexy, powerful, and fierce.

DO WHAT MAKES YOU HAPPY

In the same conversation as "no judgment," do what makes you happy when it comes to your appearance. That means if you want breast implants and can afford them, get 'em girl. If you want

Botox or injections, or veneers, or a face lift, or booty injections, do it. Again, this is *your* life, your body, and your decision. Just make sure you're not spending outside your budget for it or getting overly obsessed with it.

Full disclosure, I started getting Botox at around age forty to lift my eyebrows, and I love it. I also started getting lip injections when I was forty-four and love them. I get regular facials and treat my age spots, and one day will get the mommy make-over. I have no shame around any of it. Do what makes you happy.

COACHING

There are a lot of tips in this book; remember to take what applies to you and implement what you can. No need to overwhelm yourself by trying to do it all at once. Do one thing for a few weeks, then layer in another, and so on. That's how you build consistency and strong habits.

LESSON #17

DATE YOURSELF

How to treat yourself well and value "me time."

Not long after I moved in with Noni, she took a trip to Ireland (I get my *strong women, world traveler* thing from her), which happened to coincide with my twenty-second birthday. Since she was out of town, and I didn't know anyone yet, I made a reservation at a nice restaurant and took myself out to dinner for my birthday. I remember the young hot waiter being so shocked that I was out to dinner, ordering a four-course meal no less, by myself on my birthday. It seemed strange to him, but not to me.

That started a lifelong tradition of dating myself. On Sunday mornings I had a standing date with myself at a favorite breakfast joint, I'd bring a book or a journal, and cherished the alone time. It felt luxurious and edgy. It gave me time to contemplate, to write, to think, to plan. When I started making friends, they all wanted to join me for Sunday breakfast, but I was resolute. "Nope, Sunday morning is 'date with myself,' day," I'd respond to a gaggle of their good-natured harassing comments. "But we can do brunch on Saturdays instead." I offered and they agreed, so for two years, my weekends were friend brunch, and Sarah date. It was amazing.

I kept the tradition alive, though less often, after I got married. When my then husband traveled for work, I'd take myself out to dinner or breakfast. It's something I still love to do. I always have a nice dinner out when I travel, or when my kids go to their dad's for a weekend. I'll get dressed up, bring a notepad, and write while sipping great wine and working my way slowly through three or four courses.

I know many women are afraid to eat alone, but there is nothing to fear. It does not make you pathetic; it makes you brave and confident. It is also a great way to meet people, as I find diners and staff are more open to chat with you if you're alone. Being comfortable in your own company is important; knowing how to entertain yourself and bring joy and pleasure into your life without waiting for someone else to provide it, is powerful.

COACHING

Ladies, regardless of whether you're single, married, or in a relationship, take yourself out for a meal once in a while. It doesn't need to be fancy the first time you venture out; it could be a cute little taco spot, but take a book or a journal, order a drink, and enjoy yourself. Don't be on your phone. Read or write. It's the best way to be present and enjoy the moment. You'll smell the food cooking, you'll see the baby making faces at you, you'll smile at the cute waiter. Be present, even with yourself.

BEING SINGLE DOESN'T SUCK

How to embrace, evolve, and LOVE being single.

There is a lot of societal pressure to always be coupled-up, but I'm here to tell you, being single can be incredible. Don't buy into the BS messaging that you can't be happy as a single woman; it's a lie.

Because I married my high school sweetheart, I had zero dating experience when my marriage ended at age thirty-three. Internet dating was just becoming a thing with Plenty of Fish and Match.com, and I was overwhelmed. After my divorce I played the "casual" dating game for a few years, finding my legs in this new life, but it wasn't pretty. I knew I did not want anyone to meet my children, which meant that I also did not want a serious relationship while they were living at home. So, after about five years of dating, I made a conscious decision to take myself off the market and focus exclusively on my kids, myself, and building a career and life I loved. I made this choice with clarity of intention, knowing that once I raised my kids, I will then manifest the love of my life, when I have the time to focus on a relationship.

I fully understand that this decision might seem shocking, and it's certainly not for everyone, but it is the right choice for me. I won't pretend it was a seamless transition from being a messy dater to a confident, happy single woman. It wasn't. It took time to unwire the social messaging and pressure as well as the addiction to "looking" for someone. The first few months was tough, almost like withdrawal, but I knew that casual dating was not healthy for me. I was choosing me, my children, and my future over the need for someone to tell me I was pretty, and I knew my future-self would thank me.

I have never regretted that decision. I have created a life I adore, it's been on my terms, done my way, and I wouldn't change a thing. My life is complete; I'm not looking for a man to complete it.

But don't worry, I am an absolute romantic and a master manifester, so I have complete faith in the knowledge that when I am ready to manifest love, he will be there. That belief, like all personal work, took time to cultivate. It transformed me from a needy, insecure girl, "looking for love," to a confident woman who genuinely loves herself and her life, *as it is*. I have found love, confidence, security, happiness, joy, fulfillment, and peace in myself and it feels powerful. It also means that when I am ready for love, I will bring those qualities to the relationship instead of relying on the other person to provide them. This process has been a journey of self-discovery, which has enabled me to fully embrace my life as a single woman. Today I can honestly say, I *love* my life and I know when I do manifest my soulmate, he will be the cherry on top.

These are the steps I took to get here.

COACHING

How to embrace being single while being open to love.

If you are single, here are some tips to help you embrace it. Bonus, this work also gets you ready to manifest a healthy, loving, mutual relationship in the future. It's a process of changing patterns, personal growth, and discovery, and ultimately about building a life you will love, starting today.

1. **Identify the things you want to change.** Take some time to reflect on your last few relationships, what were your patterns? What type of mate have you been attracting? List out which characteristics you love and admire in a mate, and which ones you do not want in any relationship moving forward.

2. **What do you need to work on?** Now journal about what you would like to change about yourself, and how you show up in relationships. Do you need to build self-confidence? Do you need to find your voice and be more assertive? Do you need to change your beliefs about love and your own worthiness, so you'll attract true, lasting love? Do you need to be less controlling, more open and vulnerable, or more cautious? Do you have trust issues that need to be addressed before you get in another relationship?

3. **Who are you?** This is the perfect time to really get to know yourself. Who are you outside of relationships? What do you care about? What do you want? Take this time to build your own identity, get comfortable with your opinions, beliefs, likes and dislikes. This will help you ultimately attract a mate that is a much better fit than before, and help you find happiness in the meantime.

4. **What makes you happy?** What activities do you enjoy? Start spending your "free time" doing things you truly love. Finding hobbies and becoming passionate about your interests is one of the best ways to self-create happiness. The more time you spend doing these activities, the more balance and joy fills your life. Bonus, this increases the likelihood that you'll meet a partner who enjoys the same things, and it takes your focus off "looking" and on to *living*.

5. **Schedule it.** When you're single, it's important to have things on your calendar that you look forward to. Make time for brunch with the girls, create a regular workout routine, take a solo vacation, join a class to learn a new skill, volunteer. In other words, stop putting off living that full, abundant, happy life!

6. **Write it out.** I have all my clients who are looking for love write a letter to their future husband or mate. This was an important step in building my own faith in the fact that love will be there when I am ready. Here's what you do: Get your journal and imagine it's three years in the future, you are in a committed relationship with the love of your life, and you've just had the best day together. Tell them why you love them so much, how your life has changed since they became part of it, describe the perfect day you've just had. List out all the amazing qualities they have, and how their love makes you feel. What would it be like to be in that healthy, happy relationship? Write it all down. Then come back and read it on days when you feel down or alone. Remind yourself that you are doing the work to be in the best place to manifest love when the time is right. Your mate is out there preparing for you, doing their work too, so that you can grow together

without all the past baggage. Say, "I know my love is out there, when the time is right, we will meet. I am not worried. I am loving my life!"

When you are focused on doing this work, you release the stress, pressure, and anxiety of trying to "find the one." You begin creating a life you genuinely love, one that is progressing, fulfilled, happy, and complete. I'm sure you've heard people say, "I found love when I wasn't looking for it." Well, this is how you get to that Zen state. This work moves your focus from what you cannot control (forcing a relationship), onto what you can . . . *you*.

When you have happiness, you attract more happiness. When you feel confident and secure, you'll attract people who respect you. When you know what you want, you'll recognize it instantly when you see it. When you've done your personal inner work, you'll be ready to receive love when it arrives. When you're not waiting for anyone to provide all of this, you'll begin to love the journey. And then you'll see how being single is a gift, one that deserves to be embraced. Being single gives you the time and space to up-level you, which in turn will eventually attract the relationship you dream of. Enjoy the process.

LESSON #19

TRAVEL SOLO

How to take a trip, all by yourself!

There is something so empowering about travel, it opens your mind, unclogs your senses, releases stress, and brings new and unexpected experiences. It also challenges you, keeps your mind sharp because you're reacting to new situations, adapting to different environments, and solving problems in a tangible way. But what I love most about travel is how it forces you to be present in each moment of your day, connecting you with a deeper expression of gratitude and joy.

So, why not give all of that to yourself?

Traveling solo is a great way to test your own abilities and strength. It is the ultimate self-discovery journey, literally.

My first solo adventure was a nine-hour road trip from Portland, Oregon to Monterey, California in 1997 when I went to live with Noni. It wasn't much more than a long-haul drive, but it was the start of me stepping out to see the world on my own. It was the first building block to creating my travel confidence, learning to trust and rely on myself and how to act even when I'm scared. Those early lessons have served me well. A year later,

I flew across the country for the first time to visit my younger sister at college in Vermont, then a trip to New York City when I was twenty-two.

In my thirties, I began traveling a lot for work in my corporate sales job, to Los Angeles, New York, DC, Boston, Chicago, and many other major US cities. Each of those trips built my confidence and taught me how to trust my judgment and react quickly to unexpected situations. But all of them had either been for work, or to visit someone I knew, so really, I wasn't alone.

It wasn't until I spent a week in Paris over Christmas in 2018, that I fully understood the value of traveling solo. It was a trip I'd dreamed of all my life, and one I always knew I wanted to experience on my own. So, on Christmas Eve in 2018, with my kids spending the holiday at their dad's, I boarded a flight to Paris.

I remember standing on the train from the airport to the city and having this brief moment of fear realizing that, *Holy shit, I am alone in a foreign country.* I didn't know a soul, and for the first time on an international trip, I didn't have my kids to look after. It was just me and the city of light.

So, I went to the Opera on Christmas night, ate oysters and bought street art in Montmartre, prayed in Notre Dame, ate a baguette under the Eiffel Tower, rode a vintage carousel, wore a scarf and beret, walked the Pont Neuf and the Champs-Elysees, saw the Mona Lisa smile in the Louvre, and walked under the Arc de Triomphe. I took the train to Versailles and toured the palace and its magnificent gardens. I day-tripped to Belgium and spent the afternoon wandering the Christmas market, drinking beer, and eating chocolate. Then I took another train to Champagne because I've always wanted to drink champagne in Champagne, so I did. I listened to carols in the cathedral, then fell flat on my face walking out of the train station and broke my finger. But hey, it was a magical adventure that filled me with utter joy and childlike enthusiasm.

That trip truly taught me what I'm capable of, that I can do anything. I don't need someone else to plan it for me, pay for it for me, or protect me, I've got it. And girl, you can do it too.

TIPS FOR TRAVELING SOLO

- Pick a location you've always wanted to visit, someplace you've spent time daydreaming about and have a good idea what you'd do there.
- Make the decision. I probably wouldn't have gone to Paris if I hadn't promised myself that I'd buy the flight if I closed the next client deal. So, when I closed it two weeks later, I had to keep my promise, and booked my airfare. That decision was everything. A trip won't plan itself and won't happen until you commit to it.
- Plan ahead. I use Pinterest for all my trip-planning inspiration, where to go, what to see, etc.
- Make a daily agenda for your trip to be sure you get out there and see what you came to see.
- Be smart, using the tips I gave in the Street-Smarts lesson when traveling. Always know where you are and how to get back to your hotel.
- Carry a phone charger everywhere you go (with the correct foreign adapter).
- Use Uber when available instead of cabs, because it's traceable. Double-check the license plate number of the car with what's in the app, ask the driver who he's picking up to make sure he knows who you are, and that it's the right car.

- Tell someone back home when you are going to take a day-trip or log it on social story, so that if needed family and friends know where to find you.
- Don't drink too much in public when you travel alone; it's important to keep your wits about you.
- Pay attention when walking alone at night; don't be on your phone but keep it in your hand. Walk on the brightest side of the street and look like you know where you're going.
- Book train tickets in advance if you can.
- I never bring my most expensive bags when I'm traveling alone. There's an international stereotype of Americans who travel as being "rich Americans," so no need to draw that type of attention.
- Learn basic phrases in the language of the country you're visiting and use them.
- Bring a good journal and pen; take them both everywhere you go. Write at least once a day about what you're seeing, experiencing, and how you feel. I love writing at cafés and restaurants.

Most of all, have fun. Enjoy the opportunity to do what you want, when you want. To make your own decisions and explore your surroundings. Be open to chatting with locals, take lots of pictures, and take time to reflect on what the experience means to you. Write about the lessons you are learning and how you want to incorporate those in your "real life" back home.

You can check out my entire Paris trip on my saved stories on Instagram @sarahcentrella and follow my travel photography profile @singlemomglobetrotter

DON'T BE TACKY!

Just don't.

What's your pet peeve? What's on your "tacky" list? Don't play, girl, I know you have one, we all do. Here's a few of mine . . .

TAKE OFF THE TAG

Okay, full disclosure here, I learned this one the embarrassing way. I was giving a keynote speech and afterword at the meet and greet, a lady came up to give me a little advice. "I love your shoes!" she said. "But you've gotta take the sales sticker off the bottom." And she was right, that is hella tacky. Trust me, there will never again be stickers on the bottom of my shoes!!

NIX "LIKE"

In my twenties, I was having lunch with an older mentor, a woman I deeply admire. At one point, she stopped me midsentence and said, "Sarah, I really want to hear what you are saying, but I just can't concentrate when you say 'like' every other word. You need to let that go; it's very distracting." I wish I could say I broke the habit that day, but I didn't. It took years, and I still use it more than I should, but it sure made me aware. It also made me listen for it, when others speak, and she was right, it's totally annoying!

TURN THE VOLUME DOWN
Don't be the loudest person in the room. It's just not cute.

YOU'RE A BIG GIRL
You don't need everyone to do everything for you; if you can do it yourself, get up and do it.

NO PANTY LINES PLEASE
That's all.

PART TWO
ON SUCCESS . . .

Lessons to help you – *Be the boss babe you always wanted to be!*

In this section, I'll be sharing the lessons I've learned from my own experience and through coaching clients about success, entrepreneurship, and growing your career. My own career has seen many iterations over the years, which provides a myriad of experience to draw from.

I spent over a decade in corporate technology sales, working my way up from inside sales (the bottom of the ladder) to Vice President of National Sales. From being the only woman at a company, to the only one in the boardroom, and now being the founder and CEO of a women-owned and operated corporate company. I've also been a solo-preneur, turning my passion for coaching and motivational speaking into a business in 2017. In each of these phases I started out knowing next to nothing, feeling overwhelmed and underqualified, but each time I rose to the challenge.

I hope these lessons help you reach your next level of professional success.

P.S. YOU DON'T HAVE IMPOSTER SYNDROME

Moving past the myth.

I spent years being a dumbass. I tried everything to ignore my calling, I made excuses, I said things like, "I'm not ready." And "No one will listen to me anyway." And "Who am I to be doing this thing?" Yep, I was an idiot. I let those ridiculous voices in my head keep me from embracing the thing I was put on this planet to do. Until I didn't.

The current catch phrase for this is *imposter syndrome*. Personally, I hate that term and frankly, think it's bullshit. And I know that's gonna piss some people off, but think about it for a minute. That voice in our head, the one keeping us from doing the thing we're meant to do, or talking us out of asking for a promotion, or keeping us from becoming the badass leader we are meant to be . . . *that voice?* The one that says we are not good enough, not ready, not smart enough, not ____ enough, it's been around since the beginning of time. It is called *trying something new*. Or *stepping outside your comfort zone*. Or *LEARNING*.

That voice of self-doubt resides in all of us and is older than dirt. Don't let the catchy name fool you. Just because it's currently a trendy diagnosis does not mean it's a healthy label to get attached to. I've seen people cling to it as an excuse not to take action on their dreams, or to validate staying stagnant in their careers. But what they don't realize is that everyone feels this way when they start something new, step into any new role, take a new job opportunity, are called upon for their opinion the first time, learn a new skill, have their first kid . . . or literally do *anything* new. I mean seriously. It's what happens every time you grow or push yourself. So don't buy into the hype. You don't have *imposter syndrome*; you have *growth jitters*. And that's certainly not something you want to highlight, label yourself with, or dwell on.

My aversion to that term is its power to prevent you from even trying. Say you'd like to be an expert on a given topic, but believe you have "imposter syndrome"; it's like faking a doctor's note to get out of gym class. It blocks you from doing the things you must do to become an expert. Let me share a little secret—you will never become an expert at your thing, unless you start *doing* the thing regardless of how inadequate or insecure you feel. It's all in the *doing*. That is how we outgrow our insecurities and build confidence, and it is the only way. There is no shortcut to this. No amount of podcast listening, or inspiring quote reading, will remove that feeling. Doubt is only replaced by belief when we consistently *do the thing*.

Because what happens when you do something over and over again? Yep, you get better at it. And the better you get, the more confidence you have, and the more people ask for your advice. The more advice you give, the more your knowledge expands, your experience diversifies, and your comfort level grows. And wow! Look at that. One day you wake up, look in the mirror, and an expert is winking back at you.

EXAMPLE: If you're a mom, you can relate to this. When you had your first child, how scared were you? How often did you question everything? Wonder if you were doing it all wrong, and doubt your every move? You probably felt like other people knew more about it, were better at it, and possibly judging behind your back. A.K.A., "imposter syndrome." But what happened after your second or third child? *Exactly,* that's my point. We gain confidence and expertise by *doing.*

It's a simple formula, so let's stop trying to make it so complicated.

DO THE THING.

WHAT'S YOUR GOLDEN TICKET?

How to find and embrace your calling.

What is your "Golden Ticket"? I think you have one, and I bet you know what it is (even if you don't realize it yet), so why aren't you cashing it in? Our Golden Ticket is the thing we are best at, what we're known for, the thing we love doing. We might enjoy it so much that we don't even value its potential. It could be your passion project, the thing you do just because it brings you joy, or maybe it's your identified double hustle.

My Golden Ticket is teaching people how to create a life they love. I do this through writing books, my podcast, speaking at events, appearing on TV, coaching clients, and hosting retreats. That is *my thing*. It's my passion. It's what I did for years before it paid me a single penny. I did it for free while I was learning, while I worked on my craft, slowly silencing doubt and building confidence.

My calling found me. I was busy trying to advance up the corporate ladder with dreams of being a CEO one day. I never thought I'd be a life coach! But I started blogging about the changes I was making in my life, I shared my dreams, my success, and my failures. When something I tried worked, I shared it on my blog, and people started paying attention. It wasn't long before I began getting messages from readers around the world asking for advice. At first, I thought they were nuts. *Why ask me?* I was just a single mom from Oregon trying to figure my own shit out and get my life back together. But then I told myself, "Sarah, if they wanted the advice of a therapist, they would have asked a therapist. They want *your advice*, so tell them what *you think*." I realized that I didn't ever need to be anything I wasn't. I was Sarah, so any and all advice I give, has always been from *me*. It comes from my personal experience, either through living it or coaching it, seeing what works and what doesn't. That's it.

The more I began giving advice, the more my purpose beckoned. It eventually grew into a "passion project," something I did "just for fun." But the bigger my blog and audience got, the more it became a serious side hustle. And like anything, the more I did it, the deeper my passion grew and the better I became.

For seven years I hustled, working nights and weekends while holding down a stressful corporate job and being a full-time single mom to three little kids. It was far from easy, there were many devastating lows, but it has also given me the most incredible highs of my life. I know now, without question, this is what I am meant to do, the reason I was put on this earth. Besides being a mom, it's the only thing I've ever truly been good at. It fulfills me in ways I never dreamed a career could. It's not my job, it's who I am. It is my Golden Ticket.

Your Golden Ticket is the thing that has potential to not only make you happy, but also make you rich! It's a big risk to bet on yourself and invest in your dreams, to walk away from something solid for the chance at something greater. But if you can embrace the thing you love, you could be the only one out there, doing what you do, the way *only you* can. And that, sis, has big potential.

I see so many women with incredible talent and passion, but they are not taking the risk and betting on themselves. They let doubt and fear prevent them from cashing in their ticket. If you allow fear to make your decisions, you have already failed. Forget "fear of failure"; inaction is the only true failure. Because the best way to guarantee failure, is to never try.

Any action you take in the direction of your dreams is success. It doesn't matter if it takes years (and it probably will) to reach your big milestones, just the fact that you're out there putting in work is winning. Each thing you try, every lesson learned, all of it is the education you must acquire before reaching ultimate success.

And girl, stop worrying about what other people will think of your decision to bet on your dreams. Stop worrying about letting someone else down; the one person you should never let down is yourself. Those haters are the ones who will never discover or cash in their ticket; let them throw shade from the sidelines, you'll be too focused to hear them anyway. No one can diminish your effort, your bravery, or the success you will eventually see by taking action. They can never take that from you, regardless of the outcome.

What if the best-case scenario actually happened? What if your dream opened the door for you to build generational wealth? What if it brought limitless possibilities, new opportunities, and paid you far more than that "safe" job ever could?

Let's look at the pros and cons of fully embracing your calling . . .

THE CONS #1: *If you "fail" you might have to go back to that "safe" or crappy job, and gosh wouldn't that be embarrassing?*

Guess what? You'll live. It's far from the end of the world. Trust me, I'd rather go back to a job because taking the leap hasn't worked out *yet*, then never take the leap in the first place.

Oh, and by the way, I had to do just that, *twice*. Yep, twice I left corporate to pursue my dreams before my dream was ready to support me. Both times I had to go back and take another corporate job. Did I throw out my Golden Ticket and say, *fuck it, this will never work!* Nope, I just went back to my double hustle. And then in 2017 when I was laid off from my corporate job, I said to myself, *I will never work for anyone else again*, and I never have.

There is *nothing* wrong with a few stops and starts; that's how we learn, improve, and are better prepared to make smarter decisions in the future.

THE CONS #2: *You could go broke trying.*

OK, and? Lots of people are broke and still breathing. Money can be re-earned.

And yes, that happened to me too. Two years after I left corporate to do my dream full-time, my new business had to file for bankruptcy. I'd started it with nothing: no savings, no investors, no paying clients, no experience, no business knowledge, and ran myself into a big hole. It felt horrific. I'd worked since my divorce to rebuild my credit and get my financial situation solid, and there I was, back at what felt like the bottom. I cried. I stomped my feet and shook my fist at the Universe. *How could this be happening? How had I come this far, sacrificed this much, to be back where I started?* After feeling sorry for myself for a few days, I realized I was not back where I started. Nope, I had learned a ton of lessons, made mistakes I'd never repeat, and I wasn't done yet. I asked myself, "Are you willing to walk away from your Golden Ticket?" My answer was "Hell, no!" So, I restarted my business, outsourced the help I needed to make better financial decisions, adjusted my business model and my pricing, and began again.

THE PROS: *You could cash in big time, by doing what you love.*

Leaving corporate was a scary move for me, especially because it wasn't only me, I was supporting a family of four, my kids were counting on me to provide for them, and there were many days I felt like a colossal failure.

But now? Five years after becoming a full-time entrepreneur, and nearly twelve years after I started coaching as a "hobby" on my blog, now I make in a one-hour keynote what I used to make in a month as a corporate executive! A one-hour zoom workshop pays me exactly what my paycheck was every two weeks when I was the Director of Business Development.

I am very glad I took my Golden Ticket seriously and was relentless in the pursuit of my dream, despite the obstacles. But the best part? I get to do the thing I love most, when I want, how I want, while changing the cycle of poverty and creating generational wealth for my family.

The risk will pay off, it will. But you must be ruthlessly relentless. Setbacks, disappointments, obstacles, frustrations, adversity, tears, it's all part of the journey. But the reality of living those dreams is the most delicious feeling you will ever know.

COACHING
Tips for finding your "thing"

- What is the thing you enjoy doing the most?
- Is there something you're really good at?

- Do people often ask you to make them things, do something for them, or for advice?
- What would you be doing if you knew you could eventually make great money doing it?
- What do you daydream about?

In my experience, your "thing" is probably right in front of you. Just like it took me a while to recognize that coaching was my thing, it took me a long time to see that manifesting was my specialty. To me, it was simply something I was personally passionate about (and very good at), but I never thought of getting paid to teach people how to manifest. I didn't take it seriously, even though most of my readers asked for manifesting advice, and my videos on Futureboards™ were my most popular ones by far. All the signs were there. I was just blind. Then one day I had the idea for my book *#futureboards*, and that launched the next level of my success and exponentially expanded my career.

PRO TIP: Pay attention to what the Universe, and people, are trying to tell you. If everyone always asks you to bake cupcakes for their parties, maybe your cupcakes are on to something. If you're the person friends come to for advice, maybe coaching is your thing. If you love cooking, or ice skating, or organizing, or whatever, pay attention. Just because you enjoy it and would do it for free, doesn't mean you couldn't turn it into something you love even more, because it pays you incredibly well.

LESSON #23

BE A GOAL-GETTER

How to effectively set and achieve goals.

If you want to achieve any new outcome, you must be clear about what you want and why. The "why" is the key to unlocking your desire (*I want it!*), and the motivation you'll need to make it a reality.

Which is why you've probably been doing your goals all wrong.

Don't feel bad, we've all been there. We were taught how to do them incorrectly; it's not our fault. We were told to pick a huge, "impossible" outcome, write it down, give it a deadline, and then go about our normal lives. New Year's Resolutions are the perfect example of this. We write down a ton of crap, things we dream of changing about ourselves, or ones we'd like to achieve, then we put the list in a drawer and forget it. And let's get real, how many of those items are we truthfully able to cross off each year?

That system doesn't work.

Writing down that you want to lose sixty pounds in three months isn't realistic or healthy. Writing that you want to end the year with a million dollars in your bank account, when you currently have $58 and no insider knowledge of how to win the lottery, isn't helping you earn or manifest a million dollars!

Goals written this way do the opposite of motivate—they are weights, keeping us tied to our current reality. They are a recipe for self-loathing, frustration, and feelings of failure and defeat. The problem is, we are writing down generic, static goals with arbitrary deadlines. They are just words written on a piece of paper. We haven't taken the time to flush them out, or identify exactly what we want, and why having it matters in the first place.

We've been focusing on the wrong things; the deadline doesn't matter. *Oh hell!* I know I just stepped into a hornet's nest with that one, so before you send me hate DM's, hear me out. What happens when you set a specific deadline, and that date comes and goes without you having achieved the thing you wrote down? You feel like shit. You are not proud of yourself for trying. You're not impressed with the fact that you made real, measurable progress towards your goal; you are just disappointed. You're beating yourself up because you should have magically done better, done more, pushed yourself harder, been able to check the box and say, "Yep, I did that!" But you can't because your goal/dream had an arbitrary restriction that invalidates everything else.

Your goals should not have deadlines, dollar amounts, or other specifics (like the number of pounds you want to lose) which restrict and limit your ability to achieve them. There is a big difference between *clarity* and *specifics*. You must have clarity to achieve anything. Specifics, on the other hand, are just fancy limitations.

Let me illustrate exactly what I mean. Here's how a typical goal is written with arbitrary specifics: *I want a million dollars in my bank account by December of next year.*

There are four big problems with this.

1. **It sets you up to feel like a failure.** Because if you bust your ass and only have $750,000 in December of the following year, you failed your goal. You get no credit for having saved or generated ¾ of a million.

2. **It puts a nasty asterisk on your eventual win**. It robs you of the joy you deserve for hitting that milestone in two months, or two years. *"Well, I didn't do it by the time I said I would, so . . ."* Hitting the milestone was the important bit, and it got completely overshadowed by a random deadline.

3. **It limits your potential.** Why limit your goal to $1M? I don't know about you, but I don't want to cap my potential.

4. **Be careful what you wish for.** With the focus on getting $1M in your bank account, you could actually manifest negatively, by getting debts over $1M or other ways of losing the money, so that number you were so fixated on, wound up getting you nowhere.

Instead of focusing on a dollar amount and a deadline, we should be asking ourselves, *what would it be like, if I woke up and had millions in the bank, what would change about my life?* Now you're visualizing completely new outcomes and seeing the impact across your life, enabling you to create a plan and vision for how wealth will forever change your life.

In other words, you are defining (getting clarity) around what the impact will be on your life when the "goal" is realized.

It's not the goal itself that matters—those are the unimportant specifics—it's the *impact clarity* that changes everything. How many times have you achieved a "goal" just to be disappointed and unhappy once it's marked "complete"? This is why, because the importance was placed on the piece that doesn't matter, and no attention paid to its impact on your life, or on what the achievement would change or accomplish.

COACHING
How to write effective goals that you WILL achieve

The first step of my HBRMethod™ for achieving anything you want, (from my first book *Hustle Believe Receive),* is Dream It. This step teaches us how to transform any static goal into the best-case scenario, *moment,* or *experience.* Instead of getting hung up on specifics, we are focusing on the desired outcome and its impact on our life.

Let's take a classic example of a common goal many people write down: *Be debt-free.* I am going to run it through this formula with sample answers, and I want you to see how those three words, on their own, hold almost no meaning. But with Dream It, they quickly become incredibly personal and the "why" is clearly defined. You can do this with *any* goal or dream.

1. **Ask yourself: What do I want?** *To be debt-free.*
2. **Why do I want it?** *Because it will relieve stress and anxiety and enable me to do what I want, when I want.*
3. **What would it feel like if I was not stressed or anxious about money?** *I would feel lighter, I'd smile more, I wouldn't be afraid to open bills, I could help people when needed, I wouldn't be snappy with my family, I could think*

about other things, it would improve my mental health, I'd be more receptive to new ideas and opportunities.

4. **What would I do, if I could do what I wanted, when I wanted?** *I would say yes when friends asked me to do things with them, I could sign my kid up for those expensive tennis lessons and feel great about it. I could take vacation even if I didn't have vacation days, I could treat myself by doing _____ without feeling guilty. I could choose my career instead of doing what I "have to do." I could take time off and travel the world. I could volunteer. I could make decisions because it's what I wanted, not what was "sensible."*

5. **When I am debt-free, what changes in my life?** *I can double my investments and max out my retirement plans, creating long-term financial security for myself and my family. I can up my contributions to charities and my kids' college funds. I get better interest rates and my credit improves, opening endless doors. I can pay for things I want to do, and have, with cash and feel amazing about it. I can afford to upgrade my lifestyle by getting a new house, car, etc. I can take better care of myself, get a trainer, a chef, and regular massages.*

6. **What is the moment you're most looking forward to when you've realized this dream?** *Flying first-class to Paris with my kids!*

Now, do you see what I mean? See how worthless the static goal was in comparison to running it through Dream It? It's a process that helps you get to the heart of your "why." Its magic lies in the organic way it teaches you how to clearly identify what something means to you, and how it affects your life in a very real and personal way. By writing down every possible answer to each of these questions, your mind is creating visuals of how you imagine each answer to "look" and "feel." This process is how you effectively use visualization to begin manifesting any outcome you desire.

PRO TIP: Run your "goals" and dreams through the Dream It process. Ask yourself the following questions regarding a specific goal.

1. What do I want? (What's my desired result? Biggest and best version.)
2. Why do I want it?
3. What would it feel like if _____ happened? (Insert the answers from the question above)
4. What could I do differently then, that I can't do now?
5. When I achieve this goal, how will it impact my life? What will change?
6. What is the moment I'm looking forward to most when I realize this dream or achieve this goal? *(List several very specific moments; be descriptive. They must be things you really want and are excited about the prospect of them happening one day).*

That last point (#6) is the big one, it's where you make the translation from a static goal, to three-dimensional moments and experiences.

Now, daydream about those desired outcomes as often as possible. Think about them daily, imagine how it's going to feel when the possibilities become reality. The more you do this, the more motivated you'll be, and the more ideas and opportunities will come (the "how") to you. And before you know it, you'll be checking those dreams off your list faster than you ever imagined!

If you want some proof of just how effective this really is, check out my Pinterest (@sarahcentrella) and look at my board called "My Reality Board," which is where I've been logging incredible dreams manifested, and goals realized using these tools and my Futureboards™ method for the past decade. You can find my entire HBRMethod™ in my book Hustle Believe Receive, and all my tools for manifesting in my book #futureboards.

STOP PROCRASTINATING!

How to stop sabotaging your success.

I've got a serious question for you: What has procrastination cost you? Procrastination is one of the biggest self-sabotaging behaviors. Listen, I've been a procrastinator most of my life, so I get it. But something clicked for me when I read *Think and Grow Rich* by Napoleon Hill and saw procrastination on his list of the 30 Major Causes of Failure. It put urgency behind my need to change this bad habit for good. Because if procrastination can cause failure, it was time to say goodbye to the procrastinator in me.

For example, if you're procrastinating on getting the oil changed in your car, that willful neglect can, and will, lead to far more expensive issues down the road. We know this, and yet we still don't get the damn oil changed. This is how to manifest bad things happening to you! By putting off what you *know* needs to be done, causing a bigger problem. Can you think of some similar examples in your life? I have plenty.

Like the time last summer when I got a parking ticket and stashed it in a drawer, thinking, *I can pay that in a week or two.*

But what happened? I forgot about it until a few months later, when that same ticket ended up costing four times as much!

Procrastination can affect every area of your life, not just your finances. It can affect your business, your relationships, your home, and your ability to control stress and effectively manage your life.

COACHING

Tips to help you break the habit of procrastination for good.

RESPONSE TIME: When you get a message (email, text, voicemail, whatever), deal with it. If possible, in the moment or within a few minutes, respond and get it off your plate. Make it a habit. If you can't do this because you're driving or otherwise unable, then do not read the message! Wait until you have the time to read and respond, this way the little blue ("unread") dot will remind you to deal with it. You could also set thirty minutes aside two or three times a day to respond to everything all at once. This helps you break the 24/7 addiction to being on your phone.

SCHEDULE YOURSELF: When you've promised yourself you'll do something (workout, read, write, whatever), set a specific time to do it. Put it in your calendar with all your other important meetings and *do it*. Don't question it, don't make an excuse, don't bump that "meeting" for other things. Just follow through. The same way you'd show up for a work meeting, or for someone else, show up for yourself.

STICK TO THE DEADLINE: If you've committed to a deadline, deliver by the deadline. Don't ask for extensions or make excuses, just do the work on time like you promised. The flip side of this is to think before you commit. Take a minute and think, *how long will this realistically take me to deliver what I* *promised, with quality I can be proud of?* If you know you can drop everything and get a deliverable in on time within twenty-four hours, but you also know that it's your kid's birthday tomorrow and so you don't want to drop everything, then make the deadline seventy-two hours instead. People are much more willing to give you a reasonable deadline to begin with than they are to keep giving you extensions. If you're someone who consistently doesn't deliver on time, people will stop trusting your word, and you'll stop believing in your ability to get things done on time. But you'll gain respect from yourself and others when you do what you say you're gonna do, when you say you'll do it.

Procrastination is one of the biggest sources of stress and anxiety in our daily life. Why? Because all day, every day, we carry our little mental lists around in our overtaxed brain, beating ourselves up because we *know* we should be getting the thing done. We need to clear that mind-space so there is room for loving our life, living in the moment, and planning our future.

PRO TIP #1: Are you a procrastinator? Write in your journal all the ways you procrastinate. What has it cost you? List any examples of financial sabotage as a result. Have you lost out on opportunities? Why have you let it hold you back? Write specific ways you are going to change those behaviors moving forward to prevent you from continuing to pay the price in the future.

PRO TIP #2: From this moment forward, stop referring to yourself as a procrastinator; this is a label that no longer serves you, and we don't want to keep reinforcing this behavior. Instead, always put it in the past tense: "I used to be

---

a procrastinator, but I'm working to change that now." Use the motto, "I get shit done!" Or, "I'm an executor!" Change that story, girl; it will change the behavior over time.

TIME BLOCKING

How to stop multi-tasking and get somethin' done!

Remember when we used to brag about how good we were at multi-tasking? How we thought it's what made us Superwoman? Well, it's not, it actually sucks. Because being good at multi-tasking means you can't be great at any of the things you're trying to get done. It also means you're constantly distracted, thinking of the next task while trying your damnedest to get *anything* done. And we wonder why we're constantly feeling overwhelmed, like chickens with lopped-off heads?

The truth is, it's impossible to do five things at once—*impossible!* That's just messy. There is nothing worse than feeling like you have a million things to do, but you're failing at them all. We have work, maybe kids, a house to keep up, maybe a spouse or partner to tend to, throw in a side hustle or passion, and oh yeah, we need to reserve time for self-care. It's no wonder we often feel like screaming.

Imagine with me for a moment, that you're standing at the end of your driveway with fifty open boxes between you and the house. A multi-tasker is going to try and jump in as many boxes at a time as possible, crawling and clawing their way through, creating total chaos trying to reach the front door. But what if the boxes contained eggs to be collected and counted before you went inside? The multi-tasker is gonna end up with very few eggs, while the time-blocker can spend ten minutes in one box carefully collecting eggs, thirty minutes in the next, and so on. At the end of the day, which was more effective and productive?

I wouldn't be here right now if it wasn't for time-blocking. Honest to God, if I hadn't learned how to section off pieces of my day, I would have never written a blog or a book or coached a soul. It has been the biggest life-saver. I didn't even know it was a thing back when I started practicing this technique, I just knew if I didn't do something my life would swallow me whole.

So, after my ex left and I got my first job, I put a daily schedule in place (I share more about schedules for kids in lesson #50) that I stuck to religiously. But for me, time-blocking is more than a schedule, it's mental boxes I can divvy my life into that help me function more productively in each one. The mental commitment is as important as the physical schedule.

WHY IT WORKS SO WELL

Because it allows you to mentally compartmentalize tasks, people, yourself, your day, and anything else you've got on your plate. It also teaches you how to be present and focused on each block, which automatically trains you to temporarily detach from anything outside your present moment. When you give 100 percent to each block for a specific time period, you can completely let it go once you move on to the next. It frees up mental space and puts you in control.

COACHING

Grab your journal and break your day up into four sections.

Block 1: Before work

Block 2: Work

Block 3: Right after work

Block 4: Between dinner and bed

What happens before work? What's your morning routine normally like? What do you wish it was like? Write out all activities that are allowed in this block. It could be working out, meditation, breakfast, making lunches for kids, carpool, getting ready for work, etc. Write out the times in a schedule so you can see where your time is going.

Example of Block 1: Before work

6:00 AM Wake up

6:10 AM Meditate

6:30 AM Shower

7:00 AM Get kids ready for school/breakfast

7:45 AM Check phone

8:00 AM Gym

9:30 AM Work

Practice being present in each of these activities. When you're meditating, focus on it, use that time to clear your mind; otherwise, what's the point? When you're getting the kids ready, don't check your phone. Spend those few precious minutes each morning to interact with them or your partner. Again, *be present*. Get in the habit of waiting to check your phone until the first part of your morning is complete; do *not* check it the minute you wake up.

Block 2: Work

In this block, you are stepping into the role of employee, entrepreneur, or employer. This is a very distinct box and life role. In your schedule, put the time when you start work, and the time when work ends (yes, work does end). During work hours, train yourself and your brain to focus as exclusively as possible on work activities. Be productive during this time; block everything else out. You are standing in your work box, and it needs all your attention to gather those eggs unbroken!

Then, set boundaries with your boss or clients. You've committed to giving your full attention to the hours you're working, and you need and deserve to have your private time respected in return. Leave work on time. There are enough hours in a day to get done what needs to be done, regardless of what you say! It's true.

Block 3: Right after work

This block is the most important one of the whole day, because it's where you make the biggest transition of the day. It's when you leave work behind and shed your professional role. Now it's time to step into the next box of the day, and into your next life role. If you are a mom and or wife, this is when you step into those roles. This is such an important role change for a happy balanced life.

Write out this schedule from the time you get home until dinner. What normally happens during this time? Do you pick up the kids? Do you make dinner? This is time to connect with family and begin unwinding. You can't unwind if you're still in work mode, so put your phone away! Change out of your work clothes into something comfortable; this signals to your body that it's time to relax. Sit down to eat your dinner.

Block 4: After dinner and before bed

This time is for doing home tasks, helping kids with homework, maybe watching a show together. Then, if you have kids, do their bedtime routine.

Now you can move into "wife" mode, and spend some quiet time connecting with your partner, or quiet self-care time. This is also your chance to work on a side hustle, passion project, read, or do anything that is just for you, or special to "grown-up time." ☺

If you work from home or run your own business, time-blocking is even more critical. Break up Block 2 into small boxes where you schedule time to do specific ongoing tasks. And then when it's time for Block 3, close down your workspace, turn off your computer (or if it's a desktop in your living room cover it up with something). There must be clear-cut boundaries. I've worked from home since 2013, both as a corporate employee and as a business owner. Long before COVID had everyone working from home, I've been using these tools to keep my sanity while raising three kids. And this is how I've done it, by having clear boxes and clear roles to step in and out of throughout the day.

The magic to this system is that when you are in your respective box or role, you are totally focused on it, you are in the moment. This means the work you can accomplish is far better than work done while you're distracted. It also means that when you're with your kids and paying attention to them, you don't have mommy guilt when you need to take a work trip or attend an evening event. It means that your relationship gets time and attention, and it leaves time for you to do things you enjoy and take care of yourself physically and mentally.

This might sound like a lot, but it actually makes everything feel so much more manageable. You start to see progress because you're executing and succeeding in areas where you used to feel like a failure. You're balancing out your life by incorporating the boxes that matter into your daily routine. You're learning how to be in the moment, which is reducing your stress and anxiety. You're getting more done, feeling better, and loving your life, which is the whole point!

PRO TIP: It always helped me to visualize these blocks as coats I was putting on and taking off. In the morning, it's a robe while I get everyone and myself ready for the day. Then I change into a beautiful Prada trench coat to head to work in Block 2. When I leave work to enter Block 3, I change into a comfy sweater or hoodie, and in Block 4 I'm fully relaxed in my nice pajamas. Or imagine it in your various favorite shoe types, anything that helps you see each block as very distinctive and separate roles.

LESSON #26

WHAT'S YOUR SUPERPOWER?

How to know what you bring to the table.

Do you know your strengths? What are you great at? What do you bring to the table, that is uniquely *you?* And girl, don't you dare say "nothing," because I know for a fact, that's not true!

You have so many special gifts, talents, personality traits, habits, characteristics, areas of expertise, real-world experience, and wisdom that are distinctive to you as an individual, things *only* you can offer.

What are yours?

I think identifying our strengths is especially difficult for women. We can be so self-critical and timid when it comes to recognizing and embracing our assets. And let's be honest, we can also be very blind to seeing things we do "naturally," as a valuable strength. But this knowledge is a massive asset; I'd argue that it's imperative to your success.

In my Coaching Circle, I often help women identify their marketable strengths, understand their value, and learn how to use them to negotiate in the hiring process. Leading with your strengths can set you apart from the competition, increasing your hiring and wage potential.

When you know what you're good at, it gives you confidence in that area. You gain this confidence through working to get even better, taking every opportunity to push your limits and be the best you can be at whatever it is. But you can't do that when you don't know what it is in the first place.

So, I want to know, what is your superpower?

What makes you special? You should know the answer and feel confident verbalizing it while keeping eye contact with the person asking. Or better yet, you should be able to volunteer this information, especially on a job interview.

To be clear, it is not cocky to know your strengths, it is smart. If I know what I'm good at, I'll be able to lead with confidence on that topic in any situation. This means I will quickly and clearly be able to identify where to use my strength to get the ball rolling or overcome obstacles to get things done. I could be very unsure of myself in five out of seven categories for a given task, but if I know I'm good at two of the seven, I can always begin at the place where I feel the most confident. This buys me time to figure out the rest as I go.

FOR EXAMPLE: Let's say that one of my known strengths is building relationships with high-level clients. When I get an interview with a CEO, at a job I really want, I can lead with this strength.

They might ask, "how will you hit your sales quota if I hire you?" I can reply with confidence, "I will build strong relationships with the top prospects in my territory." They may then want to know how I'll accomplish this, and I will know because I've been intentionally perfecting this skill over time.

I've created a system of meeting top clients, fostering those relationships, and eventually turning them into loyal customers. I do this by capitalizing on my key strength, the ability to connect with people on a deep and lasting level. This is my unique skill. That's not a skill many people possess, so this sets me apart. I've now gotten the CEO's attention; they know how rare this ability is and how effective it can be to their bottom line. They may then ask about an area where I'm not as strong, say the technical aspects of a specific product or industry, and I can respond with confidence; "That is an area where I am still learning. But I know that my ability to make quality relationships will get us in front of high-level clients, and when we get the opportunity, I will make sure we have someone in the room who can assist me in addressing the technical specifics, until I'm up to speed."

Can you see how the self-awareness of what I bring to the table, sets me apart from the competition? There could be two other candidates with far better resumes in the lobby waiting to interview with the CEO, but the confidence in my strength just landed me the job.

Is it important to also know your "weaknesses"? Yes. *But* you should never advertise them. Keep them to yourself and re-label them as "growth areas." When referencing them, use language like, "I am learning," or "that's an area I'm working on." It's perfectly fine to understand what isn't your jam—lots of things won't be—however it's not okay to focus on them. Personally, I am not a fan of math or spelling; they are not my strengths, so I don't lead with them. If someone points out my shortcomings in those areas, I can truthfully say, "You know, that's not my strength, but I'm working on it."

COACHING
How to find your strengths
In your journal, write the answers to these questions.

- What am I good at? (List eve-er-e-thing!)
- What do people ask me to do for them?
- If I'm in a group of friends or family and we are presented a task, what would everyone volunteer me for?
- What habits, skills, or characteristics do I have that not everyone else has? Like: I finish tasks on time, I keep my word, I connect with people, people confide in me, I can fix things, I can lead and encourage others, I am good at teaching people things, I'm a fast learner, I am detail-oriented, I am a positive person, I can build strong relationships with anyone, I can think big picture, I am empathetic, I can create a plan, I am good with numbers, I am a great planner . . . the list goes on. What's *your thing?*

KNOWING YOUR STRENGTHS IN RELATIONSHIPS
It is also important to know your strengths in any relationship; you should always know what you bring to the table. This helps you see and establish your value in romantic, platonic, and even family relationships.

If you are single and about to go on a first date, you should write down all your assets (personal, not financial), and your strengths. I want you to see on paper what a catch you are, before you go, so you're not tempted to lower your standards or settle for less than you deserve.

In friendships, you might have a close friend who's more financially successful than you, so you may be tempted to regard yourself as *less than*. When you know your assets, you know that the loyalty, trust, and consistency with which you show up for your friend holds real value and is something they should also recognize. This equalizes what could be an unbalanced dynamic. That might seem insane to you, but trust me it's a real thing.

When I was just starting out, and still struggling to rebuild my life, I began meeting a lot of very successful, wealthy people, I'm talking multi-millionaires and celebrities. It's just a different world, and it's easy to get caught up in the myth that someone more educated, or famous, or wealthier, is "better than you." I knew I couldn't be the one to pick up the tabs when we went out to fancy dinners, or buy out Target when we went in for hair ties, so I did two important things that kept the "power" in the relationships equal.

1. I was an incredible friend. Loyal, trustworthy, honest, and real. I know how much I value those things and so I brought them to these relationships, with the expectation that I would be treated the same in return. This built my credibility and allowed me into many elite and exclusive inner circles long before I reached any level of success.

2. I never asked for things, and I paid my own way. Those are two things almost no one does when they are in the company of someone who everyone knows can "afford" to pick up the check.

Those two things align with my values and are core to who I am, so I wasn't faking it. But I also value them, and so do the people around me.

LESSON #27

MAKE THE ASK

How to know your worth and negotiate accordingly.

Okay, so now that you know your strengths, it's time to use them to your best advantage. You will never get what you don't ask for. That's just how it is. An employer isn't going to volunteer you a 30 percent pay raise just to be nice. If we waited for other people to voluntarily pay us what we are worth and what we deserve, God, we'd be stuck in the same income bracket forever!

Up-leveling is scary, I get it. It's terrifying the first time you negotiate your salary, or benefits package, or up your prices in your business. I have been there. I know that pain. I must have had at least four corporate jobs in my career, before my brother (who's an attorney), asked me what part of my benefits package and salary I'd negotiated before accepting the new job offer I'd just bragged to him about.

"What do you mean?" I asked, genuinely clueless.

"I mean, you didn't just accept and sign the offer they gave you, did you?" He looked at me stupefied.

"Well, yeah." I muttered. "What was I supposed to do? I need the job."

"Negotiate. Ask for more money, or stock options, or more paid time off, anything!"

That taught me good. I wasn't about to have a repeat of that convo. So, the next time I changed jobs, I tried it. My knees shook, my voice cracked, my palms were sweating, I was a mess. And I only asked for like $5k more a year, but I got it. The next job I negotiated a $15k annual bump from my previous salary, then a $45k bump up from that, at my next job less than a year later. And finally, a $20k annual bump from that two years later. So, by negotiating I was able to almost triple my annual salary in under four years. During that time, I also worked my butt off and went after roles that not only gave me a pay raise but were the next step in my career. This is how I went from inside sales to VP of national sales in that same time period, by putting myself out there and asking for what I deserved, not waiting until it was offered.

So, ladies, please, please, don't take the first offer. Don't do it with men (or relationships) and don't do it with a job offer. If they want you bad enough (both men and jobs), they will be willing to accept your value and respect you for speaking up and making smart decisions.

COACHING
Tips for negotiating a new job offer

Here's how I've negotiated my last several corporate job offers, and tips I've shared with clients who are looking to up-level their salary.

- Never say yes to a dollar amount that is verbalized; ask for time to think about it. So, if you're at the interview and they are verbally offering you the job and stating what the salary is, ask for the offer in writing and for at least a day to look it over. This gives you time to decide what you'll negotiate.

- If you're going for a job that you've previously done well at other companies, I'd bump your salary ask by 20 percent, meaning 20 percent more then your last pay rate. This gives you room to negotiate and hopefully end up around 12 to 15 percent, but you may also get that 20 percent without pushback. You'll be surprised how little resistance you get when your ask is strong and confident. And remember, whatever that number is, statistics tell us that men in the same position are probably already making that number or more.

- If you've done some research and learned that the company offers stock options, ask about them. Depending on your role, you can ask to have options be part of your compensation package. If they are offering you stock as part of your package, negotiate more shares.

- Other things to think about: Flex time, extra paid vacation days, daycare expenses, gym memberships, mental wellness allowance, coaching, expense account, there's a lot.

Remember, if they want you bad enough, then asking for what you want is not going to sabotage the deal. But if it did, then you know that the Universe is helping you exit a bad situation before it starts. The Universe always has your back like that.

LESSON #28

BE HUMBLE

Don't be cocky.

As you know by now, I'm all about building self-confidence, but I hate cockiness, and there is a big difference between the two.

Cockiness is fake. It's you trying to convince the world, and yourself, that you're the greatest, better than everyone else, and that people should kiss your ass in acknowledgment. Cockiness is a dictator; self-confidence is a leader. Cockiness is a shell, one anyone with a micro understanding of human behavior can see right through. It is a mask, unsuccessfully trying to cover deeply rooted insecurities. Cocky thinks it's a big fish, so it keeps the pond small. In short, cockiness *sucks*.

Confidence, on the other hand, is James Bond. It's calm, cool, collected, sexy, powerful, and doesn't need to prove shit to anyone. It is not threatened by others' greatness; it is inspired by it. It seeks to be a growing fish in an ocean, aligning itself with other powerful fish, learning and adapting quickly to its environment. Confidence doesn't demand power or respect; it earns these through actions and results. Where cockiness repels genuine people, confidence attracts quality into its orbit.

Confidence is humble; cocky is a know-it-all. Confidence is teachable and coachable because it's always looking for how to improve. Confidence can take constructive criticism and listen to advice; it seeks mentors and experts to expedite its growth.

Being humble is foundational to who I am, and who I always want to be. It's what keeps me learning, adapting, and growing and prevents me from taking myself too seriously or getting caught in the trap of praise or self-congratulation. It keeps me rooted in who I am as a person and helps me connect with people in a genuine way.

I used to fear success, or notoriety, because I was so scared that I'd lose this part of me. We've all seen and heard the horror stories of fame, money, and success, and I never wanted to wake up one day as *that person*. I had to do a lot of inner work to remove this mindset because it was blocking my success. My breakthrough came when I realized that if something matters to me, I can and will make a conscious choice to make sure it always matters. That helped me understand how to accept a compliment or an accolade without letting it *go to my head*. I could control how I internalized those comments. Either I could do what cocky does and say, *yeah, I am pretty great, everyone loves me, I can do no wrong* (and by doing so, I'd choose to lose sight of who I am, becoming reliant on the praise of others and depending on external factors for validation). Or I could accept compliments, or any accolades for things I've worked hard to accomplish, at face value. They are merely kind and generous words that I'm humbled and honored to receive with grace. They are not a definition of who I am, they will never be what drives me, or what I depend on in order to do this work.

By doing the work in Becoming *Her* (lesson #3), I have chosen to define myself, who I am, who I want to be, and who I am becoming. Therefore, my self-worth and confidence aren't inflated or deflated based on what others think or say about me. The positive can be accepted with humble grace, and the negative hits my bubble and floats away.

LESSON #29

GET READY TO BE READY

How to prepare in the "down time."

In 2019 I had a come-to-Jesus moment with myself, and it wasn't pretty. I was laying in my backyard in a bikini trying to get a little sun when I caught my reflection in the glass door. I almost didn't recognize myself—*How had I let myself go?* That moment inspired my #SelfPrideChallenge, which got me back to fitness, and back to feeling healthy and confident.

I realized that I'd been secretly dreading work that involved me and a camera. Now this is a big problem if you have a dream to be coaching on TV, need to regularly make videos for your business, have scheduled photo shoots, and generally need to constantly be in front of a camera. I knew in that moment that I'd been subconsciously sabotaging my success and blocking opportunities.

That *aha* moment coined one of the coaching concepts I use a lot in Coaching Circle: *Get ready to be ready.* In other words, stop sitting around waiting for the opportunities to come knocking at your door, and start preparing for them. It's like the athlete who works out, and practices every day, in anticipation of eventually getting in the game. When their name is called, there's no time to *get* ready, you've gotta already *be* ready.

So, I asked myself, *what do I need to do in order to feel comfortable and confident taking a TV opportunity?* This helped me quickly break down action items I could start working on immediately to be prepared for future opportunities, instead of blocking them.

I am so glad I chose to *get ready to be ready*, because I've just completed a longtime manifestation, where I spent three days filming my story and my coaching for my new corporate coaching company Centrella Co. Had I not spent the past several years working on myself, I would have likely sabotaged this massive step in my career.

COACHING

Get out your journal and ask yourself these questions.

- How have I been subconsciously (or consciously) standing in the way of my dreams?
- What is one thing I really want?
- What can I do, starting today, to prepare me for the opportunity when it comes?
- How can I get better at my "thing" between now and then?
- What are some actions I can take to get momentum moving in the direction of the thing I want?

There is *always* something you can do while you're waiting for the next door to open or the next opportunity to present itself. Use that time wisely, hone your craft, get extra experience, do whatever it takes to be as prepared as possible so that when your moment comes, you are ready to go.

LESSON #30

BE A HUSTLER

How to hustle to get what you want.

I was born a hustler. No, not the swindler kind (old-school definition), the grind kind (new-school definition). I have my dad to thank for this. He is by far the hardest-working person I've ever known, often working nights, multiple jobs, or finding anything we could sell to put food on the table. He's never feared hard work, in fact I think it's been his refuge and escape. By observing him, I learned how to work hard and fearlessly try anything, which made me scrappy.

But I also observed what happens when you work without direction, vision, or desire for change. He worked his ass off, but only to stay afloat, never with a vision for the future, or a dream of making things better, so his hustle kept him in place. I did not want that. I wanted my effort to propel me forward, not tether me to struggle.

On the other hand, my mother had the big vision. She is a dreamer without a work ethic or desire to make those dreams a reality. She's a blamer, a chronic victim. If her dreams didn't materialize overnight, it was my dad's fault because he didn't work hard enough, or our fault because we didn't believe in them enough. Accountability is not her jam.

Observing, and living with the effects of those two opposites, was an incredible teacher. I learned that the dream and the hustle must work in tandem; one cannot function effectively without the other.

You'll never get what you want if you're not willing to hustle. But knowing that, and doing it, are not the same. If you want something, you'll start working towards it, long before you know what you're doing. You'll be willing to try anything, and that's what hustle is. It's a willingness to put in the effort, even when it's messy; hustle refuses to quit until it gets what it wants.

Yes, I believe in manifesting, but my method is much different than the traditional Law of Attraction. I don't believe in sitting around all day wishing for what you want; you've gotta get off your butt and put in the work. Olympians don't win medals because they wished for them. They become Olympic Champions because they work relentlessly to be the best in the world at their sport. Believing in their dream is a big part of it, as is having clarity around their goals, visualizing desired outcomes, and cultivating a winner's mindset, but nothing happens if they don't put in the work.

Our dreams are no different. If you want change in any area of your life, you must be willing to work for it.

I find that most people want to hustle, they just have no idea what to do, or where to start. They are willing, but without direction and guidance will give up easily, long before seeing any progress. Lack of hustle is often associated with lack of motivation; *I'm just not motivated to do the work.* Listen, if you're waiting for "motivation" to begin working on your dreams, you'll be waiting forever. It's the work that drives motivation and the clarity of your dream which fuels your drive. So, if you're "lacking motivation," it means your dream (or the end game), isn't clear enough, or inspiring enough. Go back and flush out your dreams in greater detail. *Why do you want it? How will your life change when you get it? What are the moments you're dreaming of? How will it feel?*

Those answers, and the movie they assemble in your mind, creates desire. The desire inspires you to act (a.k.a., hustle). The more you work towards those dreams (hustle), the more fired up (motivated) you become. This is how you become "self-motivated." It's a brilliant formula that you'll get better at over time, one that delivers results consistently.

COACHING

If you want a promotion at work, how are you hustling for it? How are you stepping up? Learning more, contributing more, participating more? How are you improving? How do you become the best at what you do? How can you demonstrate those skills where they'll be noticed and rewarded?

If you want to be the boss, how do you learn to be the best possible leader? Do you have mentors? Are you working with coaches? Do you attend events, join groups, step up when opportunities present themselves? Are you observing how other bosses lead? Do you have a list of all the qualities you want to exhibit as a leader? What can you do *today*, that will make you a better leader tomorrow?

If you want to start a business or move your business to the next level, what are you doing to make that happen? What needs to happen for you to reach your next milestone? What are three things you haven't tried yet? Do you have entrepreneur mentors? Do you have a circle of boss babes that you can connect with and are inspired by?

The hustle is all about spit-balling, brainstorming, and flushing out the resulting ideas. It's the only way to move forward when you don't know what you're doing, it provides a next step, and gets your brain firing to produce creative solutions. It helps you stay open to all the various ways something can materialize.

A hustler is someone who never waits to become the expert before taking action. They are not a "perfectionist," holding out for the perfect path to success. They are pulling the trigger on any idea that seems remotely plausible, and they aren't afraid to course-correct halfway through if it turns out the idea was shit. They understand the reality that some ideas will work and some won't, and that's just fine. They get that doing *something* is better than doing *nothing*. They believe that none of this effort is ever wasted. it's all part of learning and perfecting your plan and your craft. Hustlers know that we create our own momentum, and that any "luck" along the way is the result of all the above. They believe this work will result in the outcome they desire, and it does.

If you're not one, you can become a hustler. And you'll need to be if you want to achieve big things. Anyone can train themselves to hustle; use the formula above and keep coming back to it every time you have a dream or the next big idea.

PART THREE

ON MONEY . . .

Lessons to help you—*Get your money up!*

I mentioned I grew up poor, but let me clarify. I don't mean
the kind of deprivation caused by not getting the trendy Nike's
for back-to-school, or having to wear hand-me-downs, I mean
eating out of dumpsters *poor.*

From the time I was five until age nine, we were homeless.
We lived some of the time in our beat-up Travelall, many times
in tents on public land deep in the Northern California woods.
Sometimes we "visited" friends for a few weeks at a time; once
we squatted in an abandoned farmhouse for an entire summer.
During those years we picked fruit with seasonal and immigrant
farm workers, or my dad cut cords of wood for us to sell on
the side of the road. That's how we got by. Until we moved to
an abandoned piece of land in Deadwood, Oregon the year I
turned nine. There we grew and canned our own food or waited

each month for the book of food stamp coupons to arrive so we could buy some real groceries.

I watched my parents spend an entire month of food stamps in one shopping trip and always wondered why they didn't save any, so we wouldn't have empty cupboards for two weeks each month. I watched my dad work two and sometimes three jobs, just to get us by. My parents had no concern for things like savings, retirement, budgeting, or anything other than surviving off every penny we could earn.

Because of this, I learned the value of hard work, hustle, and how to do whatever it takes to survive. It taught me how to make a little go a very long way, and how to turn nothin' into somethin'. It taught me to be resourceful, look for miracles even in the darkest situations, and understand the value of money, all skills I'm very grateful for.

But not surprisingly, it also caused some seriously negative money beliefs and self-sabotaging habits throughout my life. I've spent years intentionally identifying and removing my lack mindset and limiting beliefs. I had to change beliefs, like *money is hard to earn and easy to spend, rich people are bad, more money more problems, you need to work hard to just pay the bills* . . . and a lot more. Because with beliefs like that, it's impossible to be financially abundant.

So much of our beliefs around money come from our childhood, how our parents earned, spent, and talked about it. Their views shape us whether we like it or not.

The good news is of course, that we can make a choice to change those beliefs, and when we do, it will slowly begin to change our financial reality.

In this section, I'm going to share some of my life lessons, ones I've learned through endless trial and error, struggle, hustle, and pain. Ones I've taught to clients, and ones that have ulti-mately helped me break the cycle of poverty from my childhood and create a financially abundant life for myself and my children.

CHANGE YOUR MONEY STORY

How to replace lack with abundance.

My money story, until about ten years ago, was one of struggle, lack, frustration, and even that of victim. I believed that I had to work very hard for just enough to get by, and of course that was always my reality.

I began working when I was fifteen, first bussing tables then waiting tables, for more than fifteen years. I waited tables while going to school for years, many times working at several restaurants at a time, or pulling back-to-back double shifts. Everyone knew that if they wanted a night off, Sarah would pick up their shift. I was a hustler; I busted my ass. But it was never, ever enough. I'd get a little bit ahead and then an unexpected bill would come, negating any progress toward bettering my financial situation. I was frustrated and angry. *Why did this always happen to me?* See that victim mentality pipin' up? My life felt like a series of constant financial stops and starts, compiled with misfortune and endless circumstances "beyond my control."

But I now understand that those circumstances were the result of my belief system, my actions, and my poor decisions.

I didn't know any other way, I wasn't taught how to make good choices so the whole mess had always felt beyond my control, which is a very helpless feeling.

It wasn't until I learned how to change my story and my beliefs about money that things began to shift.

In 2010 when I started learning more about the Law of Attraction, and how our thoughts predict our reality, I began to see how my incessant negative obsession around money affected my current reality. That was a bitter pill. *What do you mean I caused my bankruptcy, my home to be foreclosed, my husband to leave me without a cent?* Yeah, I was resistant at first. But then, one day I said to myself, *listen bitch, what you've been doing clearly is NOT working, how about you try something new?* And so, I started to accept my role in my financial situation and began to actively work on changing my story, thoughts, words, and actions around money.

It started simply. First, I stopped complaining about it. Then I stopped saying "I can't afford that." Then I started using mottos to turn my beliefs around, by repeating mantras like, *I have more than enough, money is coming in, I generate wealth, I am a good steward of money, I make great financial decisions, I am a money maker!* I said these mottos all day every day with little hope or expectation that anything would change, but they made me feel better and that was reason enough. To my utter amazement, they slowly began to work. I stopped obsessing about not having enough and started living in expectation that good things would happen to me. I changed my story from "I am financially cursed" to "I am financially abundant."

As my beliefs began changing, I began making new decisions that aligned with my new mottos. I began recognizing and changing self-sabotaging behaviors. I started learning about growing money and began making more of it. In the lessons to come you'll learn more about all the specific ways I changed my financial reality, but all of it started by changing my story.

COACHING

Grab your journal and start writing.

- What do you believe about money?
- Are you "good" with it, or not so much?
- How did money affect your childhood? Were you taught about it? How was it talked about?
- What was your parents' relationship with money?

Now write the new story of your dream financial future. What would abundance mean to you? How would endless abundance change every aspect of your life? Write the specifics, let yourself daydream of an alternate reality; it's the first step to making it real. Write down everything you *want* to believe about your financial future, how you want to feel, and what the impact will be to your life. Write it all in present tense and in declarative statements, such as: *It feels amazing to know I can walk into any store and get anything I want. It's so incredible to be able to jump on a plane and head to Tuscany with the family at the drop of a hat.*

Then read your story often.

LESSON #32

STOP SELF-SABOTAGING

On being good with money.

Got some bad money behaviors? Don't worry, chick, most of us have areas of improvement where our finances are concerned. Do you know what some of your self-sabotaging financial habits are? That's the first step, identifying what needs to change.

To begin, look back through the last five or ten years of your life, and start searching for patterns. Have there been times when things have gone really well, followed by sharp declines? Have windfalls come and then gone just as quickly? Has your standard of living grown with your income or stayed the same regardless of how much you make? Do you spend more than you make? Do you pay bills late, then get extra charges tacked on?

Whatever it is, we can't change it until we know what we're working with. Once you see these patterns and identify several that show up repeatedly, it's time to make some changes. Start with changing the belief that causes the behavior.

For example, if you see that every time you get extra money, it's always followed by an unexpected bill, you may have a subconscious belief that says, "there is never enough money," or "the more money I get, the more bills I have." So, use the tools in the last lesson to reverse that belief. Start saying, "my income is grown and my bills are decreasing." The belief must change before the outcomes ever will.

COACHING

Write down any and all habits and behaviors that no longer serve you. If you see ones on the list that you have no idea how to change, ask for help. Who do you know that's really good with money? Could you ask them for advice? Maybe a parent, sibling, extended family member, or close friend? Tell them that you are trying to make new financial decisions and would love their advice. Speak with a financial advisor or planner to help you come up with a plan to change those behaviors. And don't forget to use your mottos and read your new money story every day.

LESSON #33

UNDERSTAND YOUR MONEY

What do you have, where is it going?

It's so important to understand your money, even if you're married and it's someone else's "responsibility." Because honestly, it is your responsibility to know what you have, where it's going, why it's going there, and what's coming in.

If you don't have a monthly budget, get one. Use an app (there are many) to help you sort out your expenses so you can see and understand your financial state. I love doing my budget in Excel because I can quickly see how small changes can affect my budget. With a few clicks I can see how cutting out unused subscriptions means I'll have extra spending money for our next trip. Or that if I bump up my monthly investments, what impact that will make on my year-end total. I am always playing around with these numbers. It helps me understand the impact to my budget when I add a new client, so that I'll make good choices when that bump hits my account.

I also have an aspirational budget that's printed and hangs by my desk. It shows what my monthly budget will be like when I hit my big financial goals, and let me just say, that's crazy motivating! Next to it, I have the "working on it" list. It's all the monthly expenses that could be paid off, like debt or any other payments. Both of these keep me focused and help me see that I am making progress.

So, whether you "need" one or not, you should still do a monthly budget for at least three months. Track your income and expenses, ask questions of anyone else who's making choices about your finances, and understand fully your financial landscape.

GROW YOUR WEALTH

Why it's important to have your OWN investments.

I hear women say all the time that their husband is the one who "handles all the money," or he's the one who "deals with" our investments. Girl, why? It astounds me that in 2022, with all the tools at our disposal, there are still so many women who have no insight, access, or control of their finances. It hurts my heart, because I was there.

I always thought of myself as an independent woman, but one day I found myself in that incredibly vulnerable position. The day my ex-husband left I had this slow-to-dawn, horrific realization, *everything we owned was in his name.* And here's the real irony, it was all *my fault.* I was the one who'd handled the money in our marriage, so it was I who'd made the decisions that ultimately left me without a cent. It all happened gradually, because his credit was better than mine, and because he was the one with the job, so it was logical the car be in his name. It was all these little decisions that made sense at the time, a time before the possibility existed that I might ever be alone.

If you're in a long-term relationship, or married, I know you don't think anything could ever change in your situation, and I pray to God it doesn't, but . . . it could. And if it did, would you be screwed? Would you and your children be okay? Do you have instant access to funds, ones that you can't be denied access to by your partner?

It's so important, and I know this might not be sitting well with some of you right now, but these are things that should be thought out. I absolutely do *not* want you to dwell on, or obsess over possible worst-case scenarios—we do not want to manifest those—but be smart. Don't put yourself in a position that is 100 percent reliant on anyone else.

And not to be all doomsday here, because there are other reasons you should be building and controlling your own wealth. Nothing builds confidence quite like growing your money, it's a thrilling thing once you get the hang of it, and it's important to be educated on how to turn your money into wealth.

So, even if your partner handles "all your money" or oversees the investing, there is nothing preventing you from having your own account, and you absolutely should.

COACHING

Easy ways to start investing

Obviously, I am *not* a financial advisor, so if you have one, awesome job! Keep doing what you're doing. If, like many women, you don't have an advisor or haven't started investing yet, here is how I got started. I was late to the game, and that is one of my few regrets in life. I wish I'd known what to do and how to grow my money a long time ago. But, better late than never.

- Get an investing app. Personally I love Acorns, I've been using it for several years and it's so easy and not remotely intimidating, which I love. They make investing very simple. I love the option that rounds up the change on my debit card purchases and invests it weekly. This might seem like a small thing, but you can 3x or 10x that amount, and you'll be growing that wealth faster than you ever imagined.
- I also use Acorns for my kids' investment accounts, and because I'm self-employed it made investing for my retirement simple.
- I use Robinhood for company stocks, but there are several apps now that do this really well. I love that it gives me the control to make instant decisions and lets me have total visibility into my investments.
- Once you've built these up, call a trusted financial advisor, and he/she can help you make bigger investments and create a long-term plan.

What I love about these apps is they have removed all the excuses. We can no longer say, *I can't because I don't know what I'm doing.* We can't use the procrastination excuse of, *I don't have time to go meet with an advisor.* We can't say, *I don't have any money to invest,* because it invests your change! And you can make stock purchases for as little as a dollar on Robinhood.

So, start investing in your financial future, in the generational wealth you'll leave to your family one day, the money you'll want to blow on that vacation in Tahiti. Whatever your motivation, start *growing* your cash, girl!

LESSON #35

YOU DESERVE IT

Don't forget to play hard too.

Now that you have your own investment account and are working on growing wealth, you can pat yourself on the back because you're making good financial choices.

But not only is it important to invest and be a good steward of your money, it's also okay to reward yourself. I believe in using rewards to engage and encourage motivation; I do it for my kids, and I do it for myself.

I remember when I was in corporate, I had a picture of a Louis Vuitton bag on my #futureboard at my desk. I looked at that bag every day and promised myself that if I ever made a $10,000 commission check, I would walk into Louis Vuitton and buy something! That felt utterly impossible at the time, but it motivated me anyway. And one day, about a year later, I made that check.

Now, this is the point where it's really easy to go back on our promise to ourselves. It's one thing to dream about making the money, it's another to hold it in your hand and want to only do sensible things with it. There's that voice in your head saying, *what about paying down debt? What about the thing that needs fixing in the house?* Listen, there will always be a list as long as my leg of things that the money "should" go towards, but, here's the thing, I *promised* myself for over a year, and that promise motivated me to the point where the check became a reality. So, if I go back on my word now, what message am I saying to myself and the Universe? It's basically a big F-U. And you know what will happen? The next time I try to motivate myself with a reward, my brain will know better than to buy in.

So, here's what I did. I walked into that damn Louis Vuitton store and bought myself a brand new . . . wallet. It wasn't the handbag, so I was able to still do all the other sensible things, but it was something I'd wanted, and I had kept my promise. That was ten years ago, and I use that wallet every day.

I've continued to do this over the past decade. It's how I bought my flight to Paris in 2018, how I've purchased every designer handbag in my closet, and it was how I knew the time had come to upgrade our home from a little three bedroom, to our six-bedroom dream home. Setting rewards for achieving your benchmarks helps you step up to the next level of success, even when it's scary.

Work hard, but play well too. Make the hustle worth it.

PART FOUR
ON RELATIONSHIPS . . .

Lessons to help you—*Level-up your love life!*

Have you ever noticed how people who are not in a relationship wish they were, and those who are, often wish they weren't? Why is that? Is it because so few of us have seen, or experienced what a beautiful, healthy, happy, equal relationship is like? Is it because we've attracted a mate that is all wrong for us? Or is it because we've never been taught the skills and tools to build and cultivate that caliber of relationship?

Whatever the reason, our love relationships are complicated and often the source of ongoing friction and stress, but they don't need to be. I've found that there are essentially two types of relationships: the ones that need to be over, and ones that need TLC.

In all my years coaching women, I have never seen a variation to these two relationship types. I know this might be a shocking statement, but it's true. Here's why, if you are in a "good" relationship, one that is (more days than not) support-ive, loving, caring, all the good things, then you already know it requires constant TLC, and it's good because you both make an effort to provide it. If you're in a relationship that has a solid, healthy, loving foundation, but is going through a rough patch (all of them do), then it's probably time to up the TLC. But, if the relationship is living past its expiration date, you know it, and no amount of TLC will bring it back to life, for the long haul.

As a coach, I am never diagnosing a relationship or telling my clients what they should or should not do. My job is to pro-vide tools that help them see things clearly and empower them to make decisions based on their own instincts. The methods I teach help us discover who we really are individually, and in that self-discovery process the truth about your relationship will always reveal itself to you. If it's "good," the work will make it better, stronger, and more connected. If it's an unhealthy or "bad" relationship, there will be no doubt, the decision will be clear.

I am proud of the fact that over the years I've helped count-less women leave unhealthy relationships and marriages, to build a life they love. I'm equally proud that I've helped as many or more manifest their soulmate, get engaged, married, and start families. My work is about providing the tools needed *to follow your intuition, not be your intuition.*

The advice in this section is with both of those relation-ship types in mind. There are lessons that will ideally help you build an even stronger bond with your partner, or give you tools if you know it's time to end it and move on. If you're single, hopefully both parts will help you get clear on what you want, so that your next relationship is everything you want (and deserve) it to be.

WHAT IS LOVE?

How to define your kinda love.

Love is not a feeling; feelings change. It's not a spark; flames are easily extinguished. It is not the air you breathe; you can live without it. It's not pain, anger, violence, agony, mistrust, jealousy, resentment, or bitterness. It is not a piece of paper, or a piece of jewelry. It's not a relationship status or a housemate. It is not your security, your safety, or your savior. It will not complete you; it will not rescue you. Love is not chemistry; good sex is basic.

Those are just the things we chase or try to avoid when we're aimlessly looking for love. They are the manifestations of our beliefs about what love looks like, how it acts, and how it makes us feel. They are not, *love itself.*

So, what is love?

What does *love* mean to you?

When you don't have a clear answer to that question, you wind up manifesting the above list in various forms, or your own version of it. You manifest the outward expressions of what you think love should be or the dysfunctional "love" you've experienced or witnessed. If you have a subconscious belief that love is displayed through jealousy (*if he loved me, he wouldn't want me to go out with my girlfriends, or have any guy friends*), then you are looking for, and will attract, the jealous psycho and a dysfunctional, co-dependent relationship. If you believe that love is a feeling, chemistry, or a spark, you'll manifest the douchebag who just wants to sleep with you. If you believe love is a piece of paper or jewelry, then you'll marry the wrong guy just because they provide those things. If you believe it is pain, you will manifest a nightmare rollercoaster of pain.

Most women spend all their time identifying the things they don't want, never realizing this clarity can only manifest exactly that. What *you* focus on, is what will show up. So, if your focus is on what you do not want, that's exactly what you will get. The Universe does not understand the difference between "do" and "don't"; it focuses on the subject of the statement, and the action item.

For example: "I don't want a guy who treats me badly." The Universe hears, and will deliver, "guy who treats me badly." This is the reason many women repeatedly manifest versions of the same guy or relationship.

So instead, identify what you *do want.* "I want a guy who respects me." This might seem silly, but it's not a joke.

What kind of love do you want and deserve?

COACHING

Get out your journal and take some intentional time; this one is important, whether you're in a relationship or not. Be honest with yourself and answer each of these fully.

- When I think about love, I think . . .
- What does love mean to me?
- What are some actions that demonstrate love?
- When do I feel most loved?

- Who makes me feel that way?
- Is that person's love conditional?
- Do I feel like I need to always "earn" their love, or prove mine?
- What are some expressions of love that are important to me?
- List all the words that describe a happy, healthy, loving, equal, committed relationship
- How do you want to be treated by your current or future partner?
- Write the description of a couple in an ideal relationship. How do they treat each other, look at each other, value each other, behave around people, behave when no one is watching, how do they take care of one another, talk to each other, support each other?

This journaling, if taken seriously, will reveal to you what is in your heart. Do not judge it. Whatever you wrote, don't try and make excuses for it, or validate it, or even make big decisions based on it. Just let it be your truth for a while. Let it marinate. Come back and read it a week or two later, then expand, write some more. Let your truth come to you.

LESSON #37

PLAY FAIR

Don't ask for what you won't give.

It's not always easy, but it's important to play fair in your relationship. Are you asking your partner to do things that you are not doing? Do you expect them to treat you with love and respect, but withhold those things yourself? It's so easy to justify behavior in a tit-for-tat fashion, *well they aren't being kind to me, so I'm gonna be evil right back!* But that's not healthy or productive.

Think about the things you want from your husband, boyfriend, or partner. What are they? Then ask yourself, do I freely give the same? Or is it conditional?

I believe strongly that what we put out into the world and into our relationships is what is reflected to us. So, when something is not working, the first place I always try to look is at myself. Sometimes that's harder than other times, but considering we are the only part of the equation that we can control, it helps us look at the situation more objectively. Learning to look at myself first, before playing the blame game, helps me see if I am showing up as my best self. *Am I behaving in a way that makes me proud? Am I treating the other person the way I want to be treated? Have I communicated my feelings, tried to tell the other person where I'm coming from in a way that doesn't make them defensive?* If I can honestly answer yes to these questions, then I can hold the other person accountable for doing the same. But I can't honestly do that if I haven't assessed my own behavior first.

LESSON #38

RESET THE ENERGY

Bees and honey.

Don't you hate it when your relationship slips into a negative pattern of nagging, sniping at each other, and energy so tense you can cut it with a fork? It's no fun. It can feel out of our control, like there's nothing we can do to turn the vibe around, we're just waiting for something to come along and magically turn the tide.

But there is something we can do that can completely reset the energy in our home and relationship. I call it *bees and honey*, and you already know what I'm getting at.

Let's start with nagging. It's a common complaint from both parties in just about any relationship. We ladies hate to do it, as much as our partner hates being on the receiving end. Nagging sucks! It creates ongoing tension that gets worse over time. It makes us feel unheard, and them feel unappreciated.

Like the Law of Attraction states, we get back what we've put out, so if we are constantly nagging *(bitching, complaining, feeling like we are repeatedly talking to a wall)*, resistance, defensiveness, resentment, and tension is what will manifest in response. In my section on parenting, I share a lesson about positive reinforcement, and yes, it's in reference to children, but it's just as applicable to a mate. Most humans respond better to positivity than negativity, so the best way to get him to contribute more around the house, or to help out with the kids, or to give you more time and attention, is to model and praise this behavior.

In other words, we use a basic formula, *what you focus on expands.* In this case, if I only focus on behavior I don't like, that behavior gets worse and more prevalent and over time, the problem grows and expands. If instead, I focus on the behavior I want to see more of, it will also grow and expand over time.

Example: If you ask him every day to take out the trash (getting more annoyed each time he doesn't), and then on the day he does, make a snide remark like, *well it's about time!* that is focusing on the negative and ignoring the positive, which makes the problem worse. It sends a message that he can interpret as, *don't even bother, nothing I do is going to make her happy anyway.* Instead, focus on the positive. Notice that he did what you asked, and kindly thank him for it. Give him a kiss or a hug, reward the "good behavior" the same way we do with our kids.

Now this might sound too simplistic, but it works. Is it fair that you are the one initiating these changes by treating him differently, when he's the one who needs to change. No. It's not. But if what you've been doing isn't working, and your relationship is deteriorating, then isn't it worth trying something new?

Positive reinforcement is the fastest, most effective way in my experience to change the vibe and energy in your relationship. It relieves tension and stops the dreaded feeling of "walking on eggshells." Men want to be appreciated just like we do, and when their efforts are not noticed or rewarded by a change in our response, they can withdraw.

So, if your relationship needs a reset and you're longing for connected closeness with your partner, using positivity and modeling the behavior you want reciprocated is the fastest way to cut the tension and close the divide.

COACHING

Try these tips for one week and just see what happens. Normally you can feel shifts in energy within a few days, but depending on how long things have been difficult, or tense, it could take a little longer.

- Start with something small. Ask him kindly, with as little negative feedback in your tone as you can, to do something specific within a specific timeframe. "Hey honey, do you mind taking out the trash before you leave for work today?" Smile, maybe add a kiss or a hug. Again, we are showing the behavior we want back. This is *not* about kissing his ass, this is about getting back to a mutually loving and kind communication pattern.

- If he takes the trash out on his way to work, send him a loving thank-you text or voice memo. Notice and reward the fact that he did it, the way you probably did when you first started dating.

- If he forgets to do it, don't say a word about it when he gets home. Show him love and affection and give him the space to possibly remember on his own. If he does take the trash out any time before bed, give him a kiss, say thank you, notice it, and notice him. Show that when he listens and follows through, it means something to you, it's valued and seen.

- If he didn't do it at all that day, ask again the next morning using the same tone as before, no added sarcasm or criticism.
- Follow the same steps as before.
- Don't empty the trash for him, wait until he does it.

That's a silly example, but you can do this with anything, just start out small and be specific. Don't ask him to do ten things at once, keep it simple. Remember, you are testing this out, so play around with it a little to see what is most effective for the two of you. The goal is that you both begin to build a new pattern of communication that is based in positivity, kindness, appreciation, and love. It's showing him that he is seen and appreciated, and it won't be long before you start to see a shift in the way he's responding and treating you in return. It is going to take time, so be patient. Trust needs to be reestablished between both of you. At first, he's going to expect you to react as before, if he does something "wrong," or forgets to do what you've asked, but when you meet him with kindness and respect, it quickly begins defusing negative energy. And when you show how happy and appreciative you are when he does follow through, that starts encouraging him to do it more often.

The goal being that how you treat him starts changing how he treats you. Which shifts the energy in the relationship from negative to positive. So, if he used to be more kind, affectionate, caring, and thoughtful, following these tips can bring that out in him once again. If he was never nice to begin with, well, refer to the asterisk at the end of this lesson.

I know this might seem a bit elementary, or a bit *Stepford Wives,* but trust me, there is nothing 1950s about my views on men or relationships. This is simply an easy way to apply the Law of Attraction to relationships, and a quick way of getting communication back on track. And it works! Believe it or not, it's not that hard to do, other than the pride we swallow on day one and two. Soon the joy of new results will far outweigh our offended ego about, being the one who had to make the effort.

★Above advice comes with the assumption that at its core, this is a good/healthy relationship, one you *want* to be in. But if it's miserable and unhealthy, these tips may help for a bit, but will only be putting a Band-Aid on a bullet wound. They are not intended to fix what's broken, but to help reconnect what needs a loving reset.

NOTE: If he is consistently rude, unkind, and disrespectful, that's a completely different story. I absolutely recommend therapy (personal and couples), to address deeply rooted patterns and concerns in the relationship. And girl, if he is violent, or abusive in any way, that is never okay and never your fault. Nor is it something you can "fix" or change. Having grown up in a home with serious dysfunction, I personally don't believe there is a "fix" for emotionally or physically abusive relationships. If that is the case, please reach out for help, call the National Domestic Violence Hotline at 800-799-7233. You deserve to be loved, respected, and adored.

LESSON #39

TELL HIM

Upping our communication game.

Girl, he's not a mind reader; I think we sometimes forget that. We think that if he did something to upset us, he should magically know exactly what it was, how we interpreted it, why it triggered us, and how to fix it. But are guys really that perceptive? Just sayin' . . .

Our silence is not the answer; withdrawing and withholding our thoughts and feelings is not going to help him understand us better. We need to share what's on our mind, let him know what we are thinking, expressly say the reason why we are *feelin' a type of way.* What did he do (be specific), what did that make you feel, and why? Then give him a chance to explain. Maybe he had no idea it would hurt or upset you. Maybe he meant it completely differently than how we received it. We will never know if we ice him out, expecting he'll automatically guess the right answer.

Whenever you're communicating with anyone, but especially your love or your kids, stay clear of using labels or defensive phrases.

Here are some examples:

Don't Say	Instead Say
You ALWAYS	*When you do/say x . . . (state the specific thing)*
You NEVER	*Sometimes I feel you don't, or it hurts me when . . .*
You ARE x	*Sometimes you do x*

Whenever we say "you are" those are labeling words; it's us trying to tell the other person who they are as a human being. And if what was about to follow "you are . . ." was not nice, it shouldn't come out of your mouth. Negative labels are damaging and have lasting consequences; using them is making a choice to play dirty and intentionally hurt someone you say you love. Don't do it.

Equally as important, don't accept negative labels from anyone either. If your partner tries to stick one on you, reject it immediately, "No, I'm sorry, but that is *not* who I am. I'm sorry if what I did made you feel x, but you do not get to tell me who I am." There is something so destructive about the person who's supposed to love you the most, defining you with negative labels. It feels like, *well maybe they are right. Maybe that is who I am; after all, they know me best.* It's dangerous. When you hear it, stop and correct it; do not receive it.

But when your partner does give constructive criticism or points out a behavior that hurts them, listen to that. Receive it, even if you need to marinate on it for a bit. Hear what they are saying. Because if you don't and keep doing the same hurtful behavior after they've pointed it out, it will feel intentional and harm your relationship. As evolved women, we want to know how to grow, improve, and get better, so when someone we love gives us useful feedback, that's valuable. Try to receive it as intended instead of adding on any assumptions. Ask questions about it, be open to learning this new information about yourself, and ask your partner to hold you accountable to changing. If you show this openness to feedback and willingness to grow and change, then you can expect and ask for it in return.

LESSON #40

SEXY TIME

Use it or lose it!

Intimacy is a critical part of a healthy relationship, and I know it's hard to keep that fire hot, especially after years of marriage or if you're in a long-term relationship, but its important. If we don't use it, we can lose it.

Make sexy time a priority, and keep it regular to help foster intimacy and closeness. I'm no sex expert, but my girl Dr. Viviana Coles from *Married at First Sight* is, and she told me, "Use it or lose it, girl!" Check out the interview I did with her for my podcast and follow her on Instagram, or read her books for lots of great advice on sex and intimacy. My personal advice is, don't use sex to punish or reward your partner.

Like everything else, it takes effort and commitment, so if your bedroom action has been a bit sparse lately, assess the situation. What do you need to "feel like it" again? How do you get yourself back to that place of feeling desired, wanted, and wanting? What needs to change, and what part of that change is something you can control? Then make a plan and start doing those things.

FORGIVENESS AND BOUNDARIES

The line between second chances and self-respect.

When do we forgive? Can we ever forget? How many chances should a person get? These are questions as old as time.

Here are my thoughts on forgiveness . . .

Some things are unforgivable.

And that's as it should be.

There are behaviors that should not be swept under the rug, some slates should not be wiped clean, and certain actions can never be undone or forgotten. But to know what those are, we need a strong sense of our personal values, morals, and beliefs. This is not a one-size-fits-all approach, because we each have different lines in the sand.

What are your lines? Where are they?

To properly address the question of forgiveness in relationships, we need to establish and understand boundaries. Where is that *line in the sand*? If we have no established boundaries, things quickly become murky, and we are more likely to tolerate unacceptable behavior.

What do you believe is acceptable behavior in a relationship, and what is not? What deserves to be forgiven and granted a second chance, and what requires decisive, clear consequences?

For me, infidelity was my line in the sand.

I can't tell you how many times people have questioned my decision to tell my ex to, "get the fuck out," when I discovered his affair. I've gotten everything from genuine curiosity to outright disdain. I've been called cold, selfish, rigid, unforgiving, a bad mom, and many other negative and derogatory things, all because I respected myself and my boundaries. I acted with decisiveness based on my intuition, values, and beliefs. A decision I have never once regretted. To me, the act of betrayal and infidelity was unforgivable, something I knew there is no coming back from. It is not something anyone forgets, or I'd argue, ever truly forgives.

However, that doesn't mean that I haven't forgiven *him*. It took me about a year, but one day I felt it, a flood of toxic anger, resentment, and hurt drain from my body and soul. I forgave him. In that moment I realized everything had happened for a reason, I'd been given a fresh start to create a life designed by me, and that was liberating. I will never forget it, I was driving and immediately called and left him a voicemail. I did this for myself; for my own release and healing, I told him he was forgiven. It set me free.

There is a big difference between forgiving a person, and forgiving an action. Not every action should be forgiven. And just because you forgive someone, does not mean you need to take them back, or allow them another opportunity to hurt you.

I think many outside factors (society, family, friends, religion, media) try to influence our views on forgiveness. They range from forgive everyone and everything, under any circumstances, to the opposite. There's a lot of pressure to be altruistic and to repeatedly give "second chances." I unsubscribe from that.

I think *we* matter.

I believe that if we are not being treated appropriately that it's our responsibility to enforce consequences. If someone burns you twice, there is no excuse for allowing them do it a third time. As women, we need to understand and respect our value and stop forgiving bad behavior without repercussion. We need to stop viewing being "alone" as the ultimate punishment for enforcing boundaries. If a guy leaves you because you've demonstrated their actions had consequences, then good riddance! How is that a man you want, or a relationship worth fighting for?

It's time to raise the bar.

COACHING

Having boundaries in all things is so important, and relationships are no different. In your journal, answer these questions.

- What works for *me?* Forget what works for him, or everyone else; *what works for me?*
- What are my non-negotiables?
- What behaviors or actions will not be tolerated?
- What things deserve a second chance and what does not?
- What will the consequences be if someone crosses the line?

Personally, I believe there is only one *second chance.* Any more than that, and we are the ones enabling and allowing the behavior.

LESSON #43

NOPE, YOU CAN'T CHANGE HIM

No more wasted energy.

Maya Angelou once said, "When someone shows you who they are, believe them the first time."

As a coach, it's hard to see a woman continually expend her energy trying to change a man. Because I know, from endless experience, there is nothing we can do to change another person. And I think consciously that woman knows it too, and if asked, she'd say that's *not* what she's trying to do—but her actions tell a different story.

I love the above Maya Angelou quote so much, if only we all lived by those words. How much hurt, pain, and self-sabotaging behaviors would we avoid if we just saw people for who they *are*, not who we dream they could be.

You cannot change him.

You can't make him nicer, kinder, better.

You can't make him stop drinking or quit any other addiction.

You can't make him want more for his life or inspire him enough to one day be motivated.

You can't make him smarter, more adventurous, less outgoing, more outgoing, interesting, less intense, more passionate, or anything else.

You can't change his values or beliefs. Or change how he feels about marriage or kids.

Can some guys fake those changes? Sure, for a while. A guy who made it clear that he never wants to get married when you first met, might seem to "change his mind" when he gives you a ring, but how many of those marriages are happy ten years later? Did you *really change him?* Or did he successfully tell you what you wanted to hear, or finally do the thing you've been trying to convince him to do?

The only way for someone to genuinely change, is for *them* to fiercely desire and work for that change. It is the *only* way. There is no other road to this outcome. It will never be you that changes him.

So, if you're in a relationship with a zillion small red flags, or a single giant one, ask yourself, *why?* Are you holding out hope they will turn that red flag to a green light? How long are you willing to wait? How much time and energy are you willing to expend on something so completely out of your control? How long are you going to ignore the signs, the intuition, the flags, and stubbornly persist?

But I love him. That is always the response.

My reply? *And? Do you love yourself so little, that you're willing to make this kind of endless sacrifice? Do you honestly believe there's no one out there who will love you back the way you deserve to be loved? A man you won't need, or want to change?*

LESSON #44

KNOW WHEN TO WALK AWAY

Is it time to call it quits?

As I said in the intro to this section, this is a question only you can answer. And in my experience, it's one you knew the answer to before you picked up this book. If you're in a happy marriage or relationship, feel free to skip this lesson.

If you're still reading, what is your intuition telling you? Fuck what your heart says! Your heart has an endless, boundless ability to love. If you could love someone who was not good to you, imagine how much deeper, purer, and richer your love will be with someone who appreciates it and reciprocates?

It kills me when women use, "but I love him" as their excuse to stay in a relationship that has long since expired. It's a terrible excuse. I get it, romantic movies and media drill into our heads that, "love is all you need." "Love conquers all." "Love heals all wounds." "Love is the cure for everything he's ever done." BULL-SHIT. Bullshit! You do not just get one chance at love in your lifetime. You do not have to accept any treatment or behavior under the disguise of, "but he loves me."

Be honest with yourself. Is that love? Is that what you want for the rest of your life? Is this how you want to feel forever?

Once you've decided to end a relationship, for whatever reason, understand that the rest is primarily logistics. Yes, it's emotionally hard, and there will be some shitty days ahead, days when you seriously question your decision, but stay strong. You got this. The reward is worth it. On the other side of this, a new life is waiting for your creative touch. From now on you'll be the one deciding what works for you and what doesn't. You'll find out who you are, what you're capable of and just how strong and powerful you really are.

COACHING

My good friend Erin Levine is the Founder and CEO of Hello Divorce and a family law attorney, and she had some good advice for women thinking of getting a divorce. "Unless there's an emergency situation, your divorce will not happen overnight. Find ways to get comfortable in this uncomfortable transition, lean on your support system. Don't go into the negotiation trying to appease your partner, go in asking for what you want. Forgive yourself every day, you'll constantly learn new things about your situation and maybe even your marriage, be kind to yourself, give yourself grace for the things you didn't know." Check out www.hellodivorce.com for some great free resources on how to get the process started.

I'll assume that most of us have ended a relationship at some point in our life and have an idea what needs to be done here. But if we're talking about ending a marriage, that's much more daunting for most women. The fear of dealing with the logistical nightmare alone is enough to keep women in a marriage they otherwise would have left. I know it feels incredibly overwhelming and intimidating, but you can do this. If it's time to end it, you know, and now it is simply a matter of acting on your intuition.

Write down a plan of action and get the ball rolling immediately, so you won't be tempted to reverse your decision. Here's a list of things to think about as you formulate a plan, but don't let it overwhelm you. Understand that you won't have all the answers, and some aspects may seem impossibly difficult, but tackle one thing at a time. It gets easier.

- Call a lawyer. This doesn't mean you have to retain one right away, so don't dismiss calling for a consultation just because you might think it's too expensive. Most family lawers will do a consultation for a few hundred dollars. This is a great way to get your questions answered and know your rights. There are legal resources in every state, even if you can't pay a retainer. Call the state bar association and ask for assistance.
- When you meet with the attorney, have all your ducks lined up. What are the facts? Write them out before you go, so you can communicate them clearly in the moment. Honestly, they probably won't care about your "story," just the facts, so don't be offended by this. Ask things like: what happens if I left today? Can I take my kids with me? What money will I have access to? Can he legally "turn off" that access? What are my rights as a wife and mother to our kids? What are my rights as it relates to our money, our home, business, investments, etc.? Is there anything I should *not* do?
- Have them explain the process, answer all your questions, and leave with clear next steps.

- Do you have a place to go temporarily? A friend or family member you can stay with until you get your own place?
- What's your money situation like?
- What will the immediate schedule be like for you and your children, and will he agree to this? If he doesn't, what advice does your lawyer have about it?

The first few months are the hardest, on you, and the kids, but it does get easier. My biggest advice is to advocate for yourself and your kids; this is not the time to do whatever he wants. This is the time to do what's best for you and your children. Think about what you want, and don't be afraid to fight for it.

Divorce is hard. I'd be a liar if I said it wasn't. Mine was dark in the beginning and has been difficult to navigate ever since. I'd give anything to have a Hollywood-style "conscious uncoupling," but that's not my reality. It's hard when someone you shared a life with and deeply loved transforms overnight into a version you never saw coming. But I've learned we can only control ourselves and trying to do anything beyond that is a foolish waste of time.

Regardless of if it is a "good," or a "bad" divorce, time does heal wounds. You can, and will move on to build a beautiful life for yourself and your children.

PART FIVE
ON PARENTING . . .

PART FIVE:
ON
PARENTING...

Lessons to help you—*Evolve with grace into the best mama you can be!*

They say that parenting is the greatest job on earth, *or is it the hardest?* Either way, they are right. It's a huge responsibility to not just bring another human into the world, but to raise them with intention. To teach them values, lessons, and beliefs. To correct wrongdoing and encourage their path. It's a constant balancing act—how do you give them everything they need, while still taking care of yourself?

How do we navigate this immense task in the face of ever-changing, conflicting, and even bad advice? It's a lot. I get it, because those are questions I've asked myself many times.

In this section, I'm gonna share some of the biggest lessons I've learned about parenting, and share tips I know have not only worked for me, but also the moms I've coached over the years.

Being a mama is something I take very seriously; it is absolutely what comes first in my life. I want desperately to be a good mother and to give my children a beautiful and loving childhood. I did not have that growing up. I had a mother who battled dark demons, deep depression, trauma from an abusive childhood and abusive past husbands, and had no tools or natural ability to be a good mother. Her mother was cold and abusive toward her, she was angry and abusive towards us, and I was terrified that my genetic birthright was predestined to being a terrible mother.

That fear has been a tremendous motivator, ensuring I show up for my children as a mama they could love, respect, learn from, and be proud of. It has made me a better mom than I would have been without it, because it keeps me present, aware, and intentional. It helps me think before I speak, gives me the presence of mind in a heated moment, to walk in the bathroom and silently scream, then talk myself back down in the mirror, rather than vomiting up verbal bile as my mother would have in a moment of tension or stress.

I am far from perfect, but I know I give 100 percent and take this responsibility seriously. In truth, I love them so much I could live in their skin! They are the reason for everything I do; they have given me love, direction, purpose, and motivation. And so, I share what I've learned in this journey of raising them on my own, hoping that in these lessons there's a nugget that helps you feel even more empowered as a mother.

As with all my advice, it comes from personal experience and you might disagree with it, so try what resonates with you. Incorporate one little thing here and another thing there, see what works with your parenting style, your beliefs, and what your kids respond to. The most important thing is to try something different if what you've been doing is not getting the results you want, and hopefully this section provides some new ideas and tools to help you do just that.

LESSON #45

TEACHING MOMENT

My greatest job as a mom . . .

I have several identifiable values when it comes to parenting, but this might be the most important one of all—*to teach*. I see my primary job as a mother to be my children's greatest teacher.

This is an innate desire to prepare my children for the world, to equip them with the knowledge and skills they will need to take on anything and feel comfortable in any situation. It impacts everything I do as a mom, and you'll see it show up in various ways throughout this section. Maybe it's the coach in me, I don't know, but it's a parenting style I'm incredibly passionate about.

Part of this, for good and bad, comes from how I was raised, most of which, as I've said, was dysfunctional. My mother was in and out of religious cults throughout my childhood and believed that children should be able to do what adults could do—that they should learn self-sufficiency. On one hand she taught me how to grow a garden, bake a loaf of bread, sew a dress, and hang wallpaper, but on the other, I didn't learn how to read or add two plus two. She did not believe in education, so my siblings and I were "home-schooled" without the actual schooling bit.

Because I grew up in such an isolated environment, I knew very little about the world, or how to interact with people, or what to do in any situation outside our homestead. I hated that feeling—that I was ill-prepared, always walking into situations blind, becoming the butt of the joke. While part of me felt confident that I could do any household task and take care of myself and my siblings in the event of a Jesus apocalypse, the other part felt like a complete idiot. I never wanted my kids to feel that way. I wanted them to feel prepared, confident, ready to act.

And there's another reason, one that is heightened because I have raised my children alone: they needed to know how to act and react in case of emergency, because if something happened to me, they would all be alone.

I remember the first time this realization dawned on me, it was a few months after my ex-husband left and I was herding my little brood through the carpark and up the stairs to our apartment. There was a strange man banging on our front door, which instinctively shot fear through me as I gathered the kids behind my legs waiting to see what he wanted. Turns out he was just soliciting, but it was the first time I thought, if something happens to me, my kids would be left alone and would not know what to do. That thought was terrifying.

From that day on, I began teaching them things, in ways that wouldn't scare them, but also made it clear what to do. I helped them memorize my phone number and my sister's to call if there was an emergency. Made sure they knew the password on my phone and how to call 911 (before they had their own phones), made sure they knew how to turn the water in the bath off, taught them how to cook, explained why it was important not to touch the cleaning products, etc.

And of course, it goes far beyond basic safety. I wanted to teach them as best I could, how the world works and why. I am always explaining things, because that's how I learn best, when it's explained simply, in a non-threatening way. Then, I always had them demonstrate back to me how to do it.

So many times, I see parents talking or yelling at their kids as if they should already know the answers, or know what they're talking about, or how to do something without ever having explained it in the first place. Kids need to be taught; they don't magically know everything we know. I know that sounds so basic and obvious, but I see parents making these assumptions all the time. Yes, our kids have access to endless amounts of knowledge, they all have Google at best, and social media at worst, but *you* are their teacher. Teach.

When our kids are toddlers, they ask "why?" They ask it about everything, all day long. I think this is nature's way of making sure we teach our kids things that would otherwise be easy to assume they knew. But soon they grow out of this stage, and just because your kid isn't asking "why" all day long, doesn't mean they know everything. They still need you to show them, explain things, tell them why, and teach them new things. Even when they pretend to know it all and say they don't need our help.

I turn just about everything into a teaching moment with my kids. It's quite possible they find this very annoying, but I don't care. Real life is the best way to learn anything; the best time to teach a lesson is when you have a real-world example right in front of you.

COACHING

When I'm teaching a new lesson, I always show first. I show them how something is done and explain why. Then I give them a chance to try it out on their own and I make a concerted effort not to give critical feedback. This is *very* important. You can't jump in and take over, you need to let them try, encourage them, mention specifically what they did right, and then give one, just one, suggestion of what to do different next time. This is how you avoid getting them defensive or un-coachable. The next time that task or situation arises, ask them if they remember how to do it from the last time, see if they incorporate the one tip you gave, and gently coach again without overpowering or being critical. They will get better at it each time until you no longer need to oversee it.

For example, when my kids were preparing for their learner's permit, I begin teaching. Before they ever got behind the wheel, I spent about six months explaining when to turn on a blinker, when to start braking before a red light, mentioning who has the right of way at a four-way stop, when to dim your high beams . . . all the things. This is done casually here and there with me behind the wheel, as we're running errands together or picking up after school, so it doesn't feel like a "lesson." After I've said the same thing a few times, in a few different situations, I start asking, "Okay, so the light's red and I'm still accelerating, when should I start braking?" "My bright lights are on and here comes a car, what should I do?" Even sullen teenagers will pipe up with the answer. It's helping them pay attention, it's giving you something to talk about that gets their eyes off Snapchat, and it helps you have confidence that when they do get behind a wheel, they will know what to do.

Then when it comes time to practice their driving, I can sit calmly in the passenger seat and ask those same questions. I want to teach them how to do it and why, vs. telling them what to do. "Okay, so you remember what to do as you approach a red light and are making a right turn?" This gives them the chance to feel confident and know the answer.

One of my proudest mommy moments was a few months ago when Kanen, who's in his freshman year of college, mentioned casually that he was so glad he felt prepared for college. "Ma, you wouldn't believe how little these guys know! They are helpless, they are always asking me some of what to do about everything!" Yeah, that was a proud day. All that hard work pays off, mama.

CARROT OVER STICK

How to effectively use positive reinforcement.

I am a big believer in positive reinforcement parenting, primarily because it just makes logical sense. Most of us would rather be noticed and encouraged for what we are doing right than constantly yelled at for the things we do wrong.

Positive reinforcement takes intentional parenting, and it takes more time and effort then yelling. It takes awareness and patience, and it requires you to look for the good rather than the more obvious "bad." It is much easier to notice when your kid is throwing their peas across the room at dinner, and yell at them for it, than it is to have noticed when they picked up their toys in the other room without being asked. Maybe they are throwing the peas to get your attention because they are hurt you didn't notice they picked up the toys? See, it's a lot more work to pay attention, and look for the good. The times they did as they were told or asked nicely instead of whining, did you catch those? Did you acknowledge and thank them for it?

Positive reinforcement parenting only works if you are noticing and reinforcing the changes in a positive, affirming way. It is not the same thing as blindly praising for generic reasons. It is a specific and intentional.

Though it takes more work and a lot of practice in the beginning, its payoff is huge. It is how you get behavior to change for good, so you're not constantly harping, nagging, and yelling about the same bad behavior ad nauseam.

For example, if you've told your small child that they must pick up their toys before bed, in the beginning you get down on the floor and pick them up together (teach by doing), you show them where each toy is supposed to go and provide positive reinforcement as they do the work. "That's a great job son, you're such a helpful little buddy, what would I do without you?" "You're so good at this! Do you know where all the toys go? I bet you can tell me where to put this one. Look how organized you are!" These are specific things you're pointing out that help them know exactly what they are doing that is in alignment with what you've asked. It's also teaching them how to talk to themselves, which is how they create beliefs about who they are and what they are capable of. Telling a child they are good at things, they are organized, they learn quickly, they are a big help, all those things build their subconscious self-beliefs in a positive way.

Then make it a rule, *the toys get picked up every day before bed.* Over time you'll be able to remind them to do it, check in to make sure they have, and praise them for obeying and respecting you and the house rules. You'll want to make a habit of checking so that you don't miss giving them positive feedback for obedience. On the days when they throw a fit, use your standard, consistent discipline method.

The biggest key is to pay attention. If my teenage daughter cleans the house without being asked while I'm out running errands, and I come home and immediately harp on her for not walking the dog or not finishing her homework, I've fucked up. She will be stung, but show it by giving attitude about walking the dog and trying to cause an argument, all because she's hurt that I didn't notice or acknowledge what she had done right, and instead focused on the one thing she did wrong. But, if I come home and give her the biggest hug and say what a huge helper she is, and how I could never live without her, she feels validated and is being treated the way she deserves to be treated, she's been seen and appreciated. Then thirty minutes later I can say, "Can you please walk the dog?" And I'll get almost no resistance and very little teenage sass.

COACHING

I am a huge fan of Jo Frost, a.k.a. Supernanny. Much of what I learned about parenting came from watching her ABC show. Her methods work! Look up some of those episodes on YouTube and use her "naughty spot," or other discipline techniques. As important as positive reinforcement is to encourage good behavior, and discipline is just as critical to enforcing the rules and stopping unacceptable behavior. She also has great tips and ideas for how to reward good behavior for kids of all ages, and again I've tested those methods and they are foolproof! Follow her on Instagram @jofrost for regular parenting tips.

LESSON #47

CLEAR EXPECTATIONS

Setting the ground rules.

Once I was coaching a woman who shared how her children take her for granted and don't appreciate all she does for them. She was quite upset, and rightly so. She shared an example that had happened over the weekend and concluded by saying, "So, I just need to know how to not be upset by this."

"Hold up!" I replied. "You *should* be upset by this. That is *not* acceptable behavior and not the type of behavior you want them exhibiting out in the real world, which they will. If they think it's okay to treat you this way, they will treat other people just like this for the rest of their lives. That's not okay. It's time to raise your expectations of them."

We've all done this, haven't we? When our kids act up, are disrespectful, or exhibit behaviors we don't like, we internalize it rather than ensuring they change the behavior.

Children need to have clear expectations, ones with equally clear consequences if they are not met. Raise the bar; expect that if you've told your child to do something, they will do it. If they don't, then it's on you to follow through with the clearly set consequence, *every time*. That is the key; you must be consistent so they begin to trust that the process will be the same each time and react accordingly. When you follow through consistently on the small things (the ones you'd normally let slide because it's too much effort in the moment to address), it is much easier to follow through with the bigger ones.

Don't tolerate bad behavior. It's our job as parents to shape our children in a way that sends them into the world as good humans—people who respect others, carry their weight, take responsibility for their actions, communicate their thoughts, help others, generally add to society. That is not an automatic switch that flips the minute they leave our nest; they don't magically become all that. If they have not been taught and expected to exhibit those behaviors at home, with their family, they aren't going to suddenly start when they become independent adults.

In our home, we have "acceptable behavior" and "unacceptable behavior." I tried to stay away from categorizing things as "good" or "bad," because it's too easy in the heat of the moment for a kid to internalize, "that was bad"—words said in anger or frustration—into meaning "I am bad," and we never want that.

Examples of "unacceptable behavior" include being disrespectful, talking back, disobeying, name-calling, lying, disrespecting property (destroying things in the house), taking other people's things, etc. Each of the items on the "unacceptable behavior" list needs to be clearly communicated, so there is no doubt when they've crossed a line, they know it and you know it.

COACHING

Write out your own list of "unacceptable behaviors," and post them on the fridge. Communicate them with everyone in the home. Make them part of your house rules.

Then when they've done something on that list, follow these simple steps, *every single time.*

- If they are shorter than you, calmly pull them aside (regardless of age, this can start as soon as they can walk) and come down to their eye level. If they are as tall or taller than you, have them stop and face you, place both hands on their shoulders and look them in the eye; make them give you eye contact. Do this in a non-threatening way, and stay calm. Your tone of voice matters! Calmer is more effective and will get your point across much faster. It also gives you a split second to take a deep breath and collect your thoughts.
- Ask, "Was that acceptable behavior? In this house are we allowed to do x?" Be specific, name the thing they just did, and always reference what is acceptable and what it not.
- Then ask, "So, what should you have done instead?" They will know the answer if you've clearly communicated the rules. Give them time to respond.
- Then say, "That's right. Now how do we fix it?"
- Walk them through what they need to do to make it right, which should always include an apology stating the infraction, so they understand why they're apologizing.
- Always finish with a hug and thank them for making it right (positive reinforcement).
- And then, let it go. Don't harbor a grudge. They are watching you to see if this new process will work, and if you're still acting upset afterwards they will begin to mistrust and wonder why they bother trying to make it right. Show them that mistakes happen in life, but if they

take accountability and do what's needed to make it right, they can be forgiven.

Respect is a non-negotiable for me. I want to be respected, I want the things I've worked hard to provide for my family to be respected, and I want the people my children interact with to be respected. This is how you teach respect—by setting clear boundaries and expectations, with clear consequences and follow-through. When your kids respect you, they test you less. When they know you will not tolerate unacceptable behavior, they are more likely to think twice about doing something that will result in adverse consequences.

But respect goes both ways. I show respect by trying to listen and pay attention when they talk or try to state their case. I show it by asking to use their stuff and not just taking it, the same way I want them to treat me. I show it by giving them a voice, asking their opinions, giving them choices. I show it by not yelling at them or calling them names. In other words, I am not asking anything of my kids that I am not trying to exhibit in return. I try to demonstrate respect, so that it can be reflected back to me.

PRO TIP: We need to stop yelling vagueness at our kids. Things like, "I told you to knock it off!" is simply not helpful. It doesn't teach them what you want *instead*. It does not show them how to behave or enforce your expectations; it just raises your blood pressure and creates tension.

Instead, get in the habit of taking two minutes and follow the formula above, consistently. In the beginning it will seem like you're spending your entire day doing this! It's gonna feel like you are riding them hard, but give it a week of following through at every single infraction, and pretty soon you'll see their behaviors change, and you'll need to do it less often. Soon you'll notice the energy in your home shift, and you'll all start getting along better. It's powerful, it gives you control where you previously may have felt none, and it's teaching behaviors that are critical to their development as amazing humans.

LESSON #48

DON'T SAY IT

Watch what you say . . .

Mama, I know it's hard, but we've really gotta watch what we say to our kids. They hear and internalize everything, and words matter a lot.

Think of the damage we've had to overcome from our childhood, possibly from our own parents. Think of all the things people told us, said to us, that left us broken in ways only therapy could fix! Now it's our turn to do things differently, to raise humans with less baggage, fewer stories that need re-writing, and less subconscious beliefs to change.

Watch words that label.

This is major, as our words can label our children and create their identity. Even the simple words, the ones we say without thinking, they directly impact our baby's belief system. Basically, anything we say as a declarative statement "you are" is creating identity. How many times have we said things like . . .

You are so messy!
You're a slob.
You forget everything.

You never look hard enough for things.
You always give up.
You are always late.
You're irresponsible.
You're lazy.
Or worse . . .

We've all done it. Even when we try to watch what we say, we've all said things we regret. I'm no exception. But heighten your awareness of this, and you'll start noticing how much you do it without thinking. It might not seem like a big deal, but when you are told something repeatedly, as a description of who you are, you believe it. Our children are even more susceptible to forming these beliefs than adults. So, if your child has been told they are lazy again and again, they begin to see themselves as lazy, and see it as something they were born with and cannot change. It might take years, if ever, for them to have the self-awareness to shed the belief and become driven instead of lazy.

Remember this formula: words become beliefs, and beliefs generate outcomes. This means that the words we label our kids with can eventually predict their outcomes; in other words, become self-fulfilling prophesies.

Luckily when something works in the negative, it almost certainly works the same way in the positive, so we can flip the script and use positive words, to create positive labels to get positive results.

When we say things like . . .
You are so smart!
You're beautiful.
You are kind.
You're organized.
You're helpful.

You're so good with money!
You're gonna do great things in this world.
Your opinion matters, so what do you think?
You learn so fast.
You are a great friend, daughter/son.
You always have good ideas.

All of these build their self-image and belief system in a positive way. The more they are told they are a fast learner or good at things, the more they begin to trust their abilities to learn new things.

Words can be one of the most dangerous ways to tear a child down and create a negative identity, or one of the simplest most effective ways to genuinely build their confidence and help them create positive outcomes.

LESSON #49

PLAYTIME

How to pause and interact with your children.

Mama, the time you have with young children will be gone before you know what happened. Everyone says that, I know, but it's truer than you can imagine. You will wake up one day, a day that feels like tomorrow, and your kids will not want to play with you or ask you to help them build that sandcastle. That precious window of time will have closed.

It closes imperceptibly every single day. It's closing while you're stressing and preoccupied about an argument you had with someone earlier that day, one you won't remember a few weeks from now. It closes while you tell your kids to *just go play*, so you can do the load of laundry that's been piling up.

It's a giant clock, and the seconds are ticking, the door is inching shut.

Where were you when it closed? When your kids stopped asking you to play with them or come see the picture they drew, or the ditch they dug in your garden?

When our kids are young, we can't imagine life any other way; it feels like that chaos, stress, noise, and mayhem will never end. But one day it does. One day we need to pry the phone out of the hands to get a response, and they must be chased down for a chance at a fake hug. It happens to the best of us. It feels like this metamorphosis takes place overnight, but it doesn't. It happens in all those small, seemingly insignificant ways each day.

I've always had a keen sense of the passage of time; it's fascinated me since childhood. It's one of the reasons I love photography so much, because it captures a moment that occurred mere moments before and can never be recreated or relived again. When my kids were babies, I read somewhere that there are 936 Saturdays from birth to age eighteen, which stunned me. That meant I had even fewer Saturdays with my kids, taking into account any weekends they spent with their father. What a small number that is. It puts things into perspective and reminds us that the hard days will pass. My motto became, "One day, I'll want this day back." Just that little thought was enough to help me take a breath, shake off the stress of whatever I was facing that day, and be present in the time I had with my children. It shaped my parenting style, as I wanted to be in the moment, even the hard ones. I didn't want to miss a thing.

And so, as often as I could (which was not always), I tried to take the time between dinner and bedtime to interact and play with my kids. I got down on the floor and played dolls, or built Legos, or swung on the swings with them at the park. I tried to remember that time was fleeting, but important. The added benefit was that because they got this attention, they acted out less. When I'd be distracted and not spend quality time with them, suddenly there'd be more tantrums, or more challenges to my authority.

Importantly, being present with my kids during this time allowed me to enforce boundaries without guilt. If I did need to use my phone because a client called, I could expect them to respect me and not whine. It also meant I could travel for work when needed and not feel guilty about leaving them with their sitter. I knew, and they understood, that when Mama was with them, I was with them, and when I wasn't, there was a good reason. I trusted their sitter (they always stayed with the same one), and so I could detach while on a business trip to effectively get my work done without mommy guilt.

COACHING

Kids need our undivided attention, not all the time, but they do need it. In my schedule, I set boundaries with work and cleared the time from daycare pickup until bedtime, so that I could spend those three hours a day, giving them my time and attention. When I started my own business, I did the same. I did not schedule meetings past 4:00 PM, the time they got home from school, unless absolutely necessary. Now that my son is in college and my girls are in high school, I have a little more flexibility because they do homework before dinner and have after school activities, but still, I try to never schedule meetings in the evening or on weekends.

And in return, my children have always recharged me. They make me laugh at all the silly things they say and do, helping me clear my mind of stress, because I am focused on the moment.

LESSON #50

OH, GLORIOUS SCHEDULE!

How to get on a sanity-saving schedule.

Honestly, I never thought I'd be one of those moms who's all about the kid's schedule. Before I became a parent, I used to mock their rigidity. But then I became a single parent and realized I was about to be pulled under by the intense overwhelm of trying to survive with three babies on my own.

Mira and Izzy were fifteen months when my marriage ended, and Kanen was five and a half, so I had my hands full (literally—I carried one baby on each hip everywhere I went). The days were endless and exhausting. God, was I tired! I moved us into a little 700 square foot, two-bedroom apartment after selling just about everything we owned. The hidden blessing was that at least I couldn't lose them in our tiny space.

My days started at six AM with one or both of my girls standing by my bed, with their face inches from mine, waiting for me to wake up. (*Why do kids do that? It's so creepy!*) They'd be cheerfully ready to start the day, and I'd be splashing my face with cold water, pounding cups of coffee, praying for my brain to catch up to the actions of my auto-pilot body. In those early years I had to get them dressed, fed, lunches packed, get myself dressed for work, and in the car by 7:30 to drop them at daycare and race to the office by 8:00 AM.

Then I'd scramble to pick them up by 5:30, get them dinner (because everyone was starving and cranky), then find an activity to entertain, and engage with them before bath and bed. I learned quickly that a routine and set schedule was the only way I'd remain sane, and I'm so grateful I adapted one that worked for my kids' entire childhood. It made my life so much easier, gave them safety and structure, and remained the same no matter where we were.

A good schedule is an amazing life hack. It's a habit that quickly takes little or no work to enforce and begins operating automatically, making your life run much smoother.

START WITH BEDTIME

This the most important element of your routine. My kids had a strict 7:30 bedtime until they started second grade. In those early years we did bathtime around 7:00, got ready for bed, then we'd watch *Curious George* or read a story. Their tuck-in routine was always really special to me, a chance to take a special moment with each child at the end of each day. I'd give hugs and kisses, sing them a song, say a prayer, then turn on their Jim Brickman music.

With Kanen, because he was older, I'd lay next to him on his bed and ask him about his day. Those few minutes each day were ones we both looked forward to. It was a time when he could open up to me about anything and I could listen without the distraction of his little sisters. I'd then sing his song, say prayers, and turn on his music.

As they got older, I extended bedtime by thirty minutes every few years. Their later elementary school years was

8:00 PM, sixth and seventh grade was 8:30 PM, eighth grade was 9:00 PM, and high school is 9:30. Those might all seem too early and occasionally they complained, but rarely. Most nights they are in bed with the lights off by the time I come to tuck them in. That's the beauty of a schedule; their body is trained for sleep, their brains and development need the rest. Yes, I still sing their song, still say prayers, give hugs and kisses, chat with them about their day, every night. They let go of the music in middle school, but the rest of our routine remains the same. We still watch a family show together before bed every day.

What that schedule also did, was give me some quiet time. Especially when the kids were young, I counted on that time each day. It was the first time I'd sat down in hours; it was time for a glass of wine, a show, or time to catch up on housework. It was also the time that I wrote.

I started writing in 2009 when I started my blog *Thoughts. Stories. Life*. It was how I processed what I was going through, eventually becoming the avenue for me to become a writer. It's where I flushed out my methods for manifesting and success, where I shared my struggles and my dreams, and it's how I first stumbled into life coaching. That wasn't something I'd ever planned or imagined doing, but because I was blogging consistently, sharing how I was changing my life, readers began to ask for advice and slowly I started giving it. Initially I was shocked when they'd take my advice and get results, then over the years I started taking it more seriously. I started creating my own methods and testing them, and they worked.

None of that would have been possible, and I would not be here today writing this book, if I did not implement and stick to a schedule. I would have never had the time or energy to start that blog or write, if my kids didn't have set bedtimes. Our routine gave me the time in the evening to write my first book, while parenting alone and having a full-time job. And my second, while I balanced starting a business and parenting.

COACHING

Start a bedtime routine *today* if you don't have one already. If you have small kids who fight this, or babies who struggle to sleep on their own, watch Supernanny episodes about sleep training and bedtimes. All my tricks, I learned from her! It's helpful to see how a routine like this is practically implemented and how the kids respond to consistency. I've since coached many mothers on how to set a solid bedtime routine. Even with kids and babies who refused to go to sleep, it really does work, and it's a lifesaver for you, Mama. Again, Jo Frost is a master at teaching sleep training: much of what I learned, I got from watching her show, so check out her tips for more specifics on the topic.

PRO TIP: Use the time a routine gives you wisely. When your kids have early, set bedtimes, you should gain a few hours each day of quiet. Use it to connect in a meaningful way with your spouse or partner. Use it for self-care time. Or double-hustle time, to get that passion project off the ground. Or, just binge *Housewives* for a few hours—nothing wrong with that either. Balance is everything.

LESSON #51

DINNER TIME

How to make dinner time special.

What's dinnertime like in your house? It has changed a lot for us over the years. When the kids were small and I worked in corporate, dinner was all about trying to get food on the table before everyone melted down, a race against the clock.

But as they got older, it's become the highlight of the day.

I started bringing them in the kitchen a few nights a week when the girls were about five, and gave them little jobs. Together we'd make tacos or lasagna or cowboy spaghetti. I found they were eager helpers when given a specific task, and that helping gave them pride and a sense of ownership, which made them better eaters.

It's always been important to me that we sit down at the table and eat as a family, which has helped make dinnertime one of our favorite times of the day now that my kids are teenagers. The table is one place where no one is on their phone, and we have to talk like real people; it's so refreshing!

Cooking used to be a means to an end for me, but after our trip to Italy in 2016, I saw what an important role food and family play in the Italian culture, and I craved it. I came back with a zealous dream of bringing that sense of love, magic, food, and family to our table, and have been cooking ever since. It's become a passion and joy for me, something that relieves stress and brings my family together each evening. I'm so glad I started this tradition when the kids were young and have stuck to it, because now it's the best part of the day. Nothing feels better than garlic and onions browning in olive oil on the stove, and hearing my kids talking and hanging out while I cook. That is my bliss.

LESSON #52

CALM THE VIBE

Set the energy for your home.

The vibe in your home is no small thing; it's affecting how family members interact, the stress and energy levels and overall mental wellbeing of everyone in the home. For this reason, if you were to come to my house, you'd never see the TV on or chaos raining down. Instead, there'd be a few scented candles lit, spa music soft in the background, lights dimmed, some fresh flowers on the table. This probably sounds like a bullshit act I'd put on for company or write about to make myself look good. But I kid you not, any day of the week if you walked into my house, that is what you'd find. It doesn't mean the house would be perfectly clean (my room definitely would not be), or that everything is always peachy, but it does mean that I make a point to set the mood for our home and have since my kids were babies. This is all they know.

I do this for a reason. The "no TV" rule means there is never useless background noise, so no one needs to compete for volume or attention if they're talking. The TV is only on in our house when we are sitting down watching something, that's it. In its place is calming music. I like the Pandora spa station, which I keep on a low volume because it immediately brings a calming energy and encourages the kids to linger and chat while I make dinner. The candles make it feel and smell like home, as do the flowers. These simple elements have been consistent in our home no matter where we've lived; they are also ones that are easy to take with us when traveling, to make any place feel like home.

From the time my kids were born, through elementary school, I played a Jim Brickman (solo pianist) CD for them at bedtime, the same one every night. It was their "night night music," and it was baby crack! The minute I pressed play, the kids would settle down, even if it had been a hard day or they were sick and fussy. When that music started, they immediately soothed and would fall asleep quickly. The bonus effect was this worked anywhere, so I'd take it in the car and play it when I wanted them to take a nap. When we started flying, I'd play it in their headphones at takeoff or during turbulence, and they'd instantly calm. And one day, when the girls were five and Kanen ten, I took them to a Jim Brickman concert; as soon as their "night night song" came on, I looked over and all three of them were sound asleep!

COACHING

What's the vibe like in your house? If it feels loud, chaotic, and out of control, try the above tips, you will be shocked at how well they work at calming everyone. And don't forget to turn the lights down; having every light on in the house adds to that angst energy. Try these tips every day for a week and see what happens. Remember, TV off unless you're actually sitting down watching it.

LESSON #53

PAY YOUR KIDS

Teach good money habits young.

This might be one of the best things I've done as a parent. Growing up poor instilled in me a fear of money and a lack mindset. I watched my parents live paycheck to paycheck, scramble to find food, and do any odd job to keep gas in the car and a roof over our heads. Their relationship with money was toxic and fear-based, and it was all I knew. I saw them make poor choices and I desperately wanted to make better ones but didn't know how. Consequently, when I was fifteen and started bussing tables, making my own money, I began to spend it as fast as it came in, exactly as my parents had done.

I was desperate to break the cycle and teach my kids how to have a positive relationship with money. I went about doing this in several ways . . .

#1. SAY, "NOT RIGHT NOW"

First, I watched how I referenced money when my kids were small. Instead of saying "I can't afford it" as a reason not to buy the toy they were begging for in Target, I'd say, "Not today, honey, but if you still want it on Friday, we can come back and get it." I knew that Friday was payday and that they'd likely forget about it the second we left the store. But if they didn't, we'd come back Friday, and I'd buy it for them. I would hand them the money explaining how much it cost and how much money I'd just given them, then make them hand it to the cashier. This taught them to get past the instant gratification urge and to learn how to wait for what they wanted. It also taught them about the value of money, giving them confidence to interact with the cashier. This was our process from the time they were about two, until about seven.

#2. PAY THEM

Then I started paying them. They could make money through their weekly chores, but they could also make bonus money by doing extra things, such as cleaning the car, washing the dog, cleaning the house, doing the laundry. By pricing out various chores, they learned some important lessons early on.

1. That they should be compensated for their work. I did not want to raise martyrs or women who would not know their worth, who couldn't negotiate adequate compensation. I believed if they provided value (cleaning the house was very valuable to me!), then they should be paid.
2. If they wanted something and didn't have enough money, they could easily figure out which chore would pay them the amount needed for their purchase. Understanding that money is earned.

Now I will say that I pay them rather generously, not overly so, but I'm not cheap either. I think about what it would cost to take the dog to the groomer and if my son does as good of a job, he should make at least half (or more) of what I'd pay a groomer, right? This means they regularly have money; they know what it feels like to earn, have, and grow money. They do not know lack the way I did. It also means they have agency and can purchase things they want without always having to ask for it; this is empowering. They are learning not to depend on someone else for their financial security.

#3. MAKE THEM SAVE

We have a 50 percent rule in our house. They can spend 50 percent of any money they receive on anything they want; the other 50 percent they must save. I have drilled into them that they should *never* run their savings down to nothing, and they are not allowed to take out more than 50 percent from it for any single purchase. In addition, if they finish each month with at least 50 percent of their earnings unspent, they will earn a "growing money bonus." This is how I've taught them about investing, growing their money, and making wise choices. The stress, anxiety, and fear that comes with a lack money mindset is one that is incredibly difficult to change, and I never want them to know anything about it. Succeeding at this will break the cycle.

When Kanen was old enough, I set him up with Robinhood and Acorns financial services platforms and he began investing his savings and has maxed out his retirement account each year since. He is excited about investing (he's a finance major) and understands that he's building generational wealth that will ensure he doesn't have the same struggles with money I had in his early childhood. I'll do the same with my girls when they are old enough to get their own investment accounts.

Bottom line, you'll be spending money on your kids pretty much every day for at least two decades. I'd rather pay them, and teach them how to manage their money, than do it all and have them financially dependent on me or someone else for the rest of their life.

LESSON #54

TAKE A ROAD TRIP

Tips for getting out there with your kids.

I didn't grow up going on vacation. In, fact I doubt I ever heard the word as a child. My first flight was a ticket I bought myself to visit an aunt in Los Angeles when I was twenty-one. Vacations were for the rich, and we were poor, so it never crossed my mind that it could ever be a possibility, *for me.*

In my childhood, travel was a means of getting from point A to point B when you left your home. It was for the purpose of visiting someone, or attending an event. My mother was quite spontaneous and would frequently, and randomly, decide it was time to pile in the car and take a ten-hour road trip to California, from our remote home in rural Oregon. A mere few hours would pass from the time of her idea, to pulling out the driveway, us kids thrilled by the possibility of adventure and reuniting with family or friends upon arrival. My mother, who was undiagnosed bipolar in my childhood, would be euphoric, talking incessantly about how wonderful the trip would be, and it was hard not to feel her jubilation.

This, combined with stories told in reverence by my father and his siblings, of how in their childhood my Noni would pack the station wagon and camp trailer to take her six children skiing and camping, by herself, created a longing in me for adventure. Noni believed strongly in the value of travel and instilled this in all her children, encouraging them to take gap years and study abroad. Even my father, who worked odd jobs and had only a high school education, had spent a year backpacking through Europe. I began to foster a dream of going to Europe one day myself, and especially Italy, the ancestral home of my grandfather.

But still I fought the belief that travel was only for the wealthy, and up to the point of my divorce in 2008, I'd only been to a handful of US states and two countries, Tahiti for our honeymoon and Mexico for our five-year wedding anniversary. My then-husband did not like traveling or being outside his comfort zone, and so I let my dreams of seeing the world fade.

When I became a single parent, I thought a lot about the values I wanted to pass on to my children and what I wished for their childhood, and travel was at the top of that list. But I was broke, barely making it from paycheck to paycheck. Yet still I'd scrape together gas money and load the kids in the car for the two-hour drive to Cannon Beach, our favorite spot on the Oregon Coast. Mira and Izzy were just twenty months old and Kanen barely six. We'd spend all day making sandcastles and eating the PB&J sandwiches I'd packed and head home as the sun went down over Haystack Rock.

My first major solo road trip with my kids was when the girls were just two years old. I loaded them in the car at bedtime and drove nine hours through the night, over remote mountain passes from Portland to Monterey, California to see Noni. That began our family tradition and every year we've taken a road trip, some just a hundred miles from home, others five or six hundred. And unsurprisingly, I've learned a lot!

TIPS FOR ROADTRIPPING WITH KIDS

#1. DRIVE THROUGH THE NIGHT

If you have young kids, they'll get bored easily, and when they're bored, they are cranky! So, make sure you are well rested, feed everyone dinner, and then leave the house in the evening around six or seven (or a few hours before dark). This makes the first hour or two fun and adventurous but ensures they will fall asleep quickly, and ideally sleep through the night while you drive. Then when they wake up, you can stop for breakfast and be that much closer (or at) your destination.

#2. PACK LOTS OF FOOD AND WATER

I learned this the hard way as a kid—you never know when a perfectly good car will start having issues, or when you find yourself an hour or two between towns, so be prepared. I like to pack big water bottles for everyone and then 2 to 3 gallons of water in the back of the car just in case. Also, don't forget lots of paper towels, trash bags, and baby wipes to clean sticky hands.

#3. KEEP THE GAS TANK FULL!

Another lesson learned from my childhood, fill up the gas tank every chance you get! As a kid, we were stranded on the side of the road with an empty tank as a regular occurrence. And my scariest moment as a parent was driving at night on a coastal highway not realizing that all the little towns closed early. It's terrifying to be a mom alone with three little kids with an empty gas tank on a narrow two-lane highway. Thankfully, I rolled into a station on fumes, but I've never been so nervous. Always better to be safe and fill up that tank.

#4. STOP TO EXPLORE

I like to stop in little towns on our road trips and find local places the kids will enjoy for a treat, or lunch/dinner, like an old-fashioned drive-in hamburger joint. Or a park or creek where they can run around and burn off cooped-up energy.

#5. DO A FAMILY ACTIVITY

Mom, you've gotta participate too. Don't just tune the kids out; be part of their experience, make memories. We've listened to audiobooks, played the "barn game" (whoever is first to spot the barn gets ten points; cows are worth five), played the license plate game (whoever finds the most plates with different states wins a treat), and practiced our Italian together listening to the prompts on an app. One of our favorite games was to imagine the life of the people who lived in the houses and small towns we passed. *Who were they? What did they do for work? What was their life like?* We'd make up all kinds of fun stories with each child eagerly participating.

#6. LIMIT SCREENTIME

It's much easier to just hand your kid the iPad and have them watch hours of movies or play games the entire trip; the harder thing is to engage them and use the time for family bonding. But I promise, it is worth it. When we road trip, everyone is allowed screen time for about ninety minutes (time to watch a movie on their device), then everyone must pass them up front and we go an entire hour without. During that time, we listen to music, talk, point out cool sights along the way, interact with each other, or they take a nap. Yes, my kids protested too. But if you are serious about enforcing the road trip rules, they get used to it and will complain less and engage more on those breaks. It's super important that everyone in the car takes those unplug breaks or else this doesn't work. These trips have been a way our family looks forward to bonding and connecting and even now, when my kids are in high school and college, they love a good road trip with mama.

#7. GIVE THEM RESPONSIBILITY

I've found that kids love being helpful when they feel their help is needed, wanted, and appreciated. So, I assign various helpful roles to each kid, roles they own with pride.

When Kanen was about ten or eleven, I taught him how to pack a car for a road trip. This was something my father always did, and a skill I felt would be good for him to learn as a little man. First, I showed him how and explained why I did things a certain way. Then I let him do it from that point on, and it became something he took pride in and was quite good at. As he got older, he became the designated navigator, the one to put the addresses in my phone and give me turn by turn directions (before Siri started doing it). When Mira and Izzy were about six, I started teaching them how to watch for road signs to know how far it was to our destination, how to doublecheck a hotel room to be sure we didn't leave anything behind, put them on "trash duty" (car trash police), and gave everyone a turn at being the DJ and picking the family movie, the one I'd play through the car system so they could all watch together.

#8. ALWAYS PRAISE GOOD BEHAVIOR

Acknowledge when your kids are behaving, listening, obeying, and getting along. Be understanding. Even adults get fussy after being in the car for hours, so try to be kind (even when you're losing patience), realize that it's asking a lot of them to be still for hours on end. Reinforce how proud you are, that they are stepping up to the challenge and allowing the family to have a nice trip. Praise can go a very long way to achieving peace and happiness on long rides.

COACHING

Don't be afraid to get out there and road trip with your kids, even if you are a single mom. It's so worth it. The memories you build and the self-confidence it gives both you and your children is incredible. Where can you go within a few hours' drive, to experience something new? What city or beach is several hours' drive? When's the last time you packed up the car and went? Use these tips and get out there!

LESSON #55

BE A GLOBETROTTER

How to travel internationally with your babies.

In 2016 I took my three children on a trip of a lifetime to Italy, our first international adventure. People thought I was crazy, and honestly, I was nervous, having never been to Europe myself. Thankfully, my lifelong love for Italy outweighed the fear. But it was an ambitious trip. At the time, my twin daughters were just nine years old, my son thirteen, and here I was traveling across the world with them, *alone*.

As I began planning our trip, it dawned on me that young children might not be as enchanted by Italy as adults, which presented a big problem. The last thing I wanted, after twenty years of fantasizing about Italy, was to arrive with three cranky, disinterested kids.

So, I tried imagining it through their eyes . . .

To me, the Colosseum in Rome would be like stepping onto the set of *Roman Holiday*, not to mention all that *real* history. To them, *a giant circle of bricks without a top!* To me, floating down the Grand Canal would bring my favorite Italy movie (*Only You*) to life. To them, we'd be floating down a stinky river, looking at decrepit decaying buildings. Just the possibility of these varying viewpoints was enough to make my soul ache; I couldn't risk it. I needed them to love it too. I wanted them to see the magic and feel the wonder, and there was only one way to get them truly engaged and excited, make it *their thing too.*

So, I decided to let my kids plan the trip! As it turned out, this was one of the best decisions I made, one that paid off in magical and unexpected ways. And before you dismiss it as pure madness, hear me out. This is how I executed my crazy idea . . .

#1. EXPOSURE

First, I needed them to *see* what Italy was all about, what it looked like, so they'd know what to expect. I began showing them every movie I could find that was filmed in Italy. Some of our favorites are: *Only You, Roman Holiday, Under the Tuscan Sun, Letters to Juliette,* and the animated movie *Luca.* This way, they'd recognize the landmarks, countryside, and even food, so it wouldn't seem so different, intimidating, or scary.

#2. MAKE IT FUN

In preparation for our trip, I had each of my kids download the Duolingo language app and created several contests to help them get excited about learning key Italian words and phrases.

1. Whoever passed the most levels in the app before departure would win $100 spending money in Italy.
2. Whoever used the words they learned most often in our daily life could also win $100.
3. Whoever spent at least thirty minutes a day, every day could win $100.

These contests were incredible motivators. A little parent tip—I picked ones I knew each of the kids would excel at. This meant that all three won spending money, learned a language, and built their confidence. To this day, we still use Italian words in our daily life.

#3. EMPOWER THEM

Because I wanted them to feel like this was their trip too, I assigned each kid a region. I knew we'd be making three big stops/stays on our Italian adventure, so I let each child plan what we'd do at each destination. My daughter Izzy had Venice, Mira had Tuscany, and my son Kanen had Rome.

Now you're probably thinking, *what? Is she nuts? I'm not letting children plan such a big, expensive trip!* But—and here's the genius part—their task was to research the area by going on Google to find the ten best things to do in each region, and yes parents, it's going to include the ten things you wanted to do. As part of their research, they needed to write down five facts about each destination; this gave them knowledge they'd proudly share when we visited those sites.

Then, they had to go on Pinterest to find pictures for each experience, places, location, etc., and present it to the family. We then voted as a family on three things we all wanted to do, with the kid in charge picking the fourth. In doing these little tasks, Italy began to come alive for my children. They could imagine it, visualize it, get excited about it.

Mira's "fourth pick" became the highlight of our entire trip. She insisted we drive (three hours) to the mineral baths in Saturnia, Tuscany, because she'd loved the photos on Pinterest, and it was a magical experience I will cherish for the rest of my life.

#4. GIVE THEM RESPONSIBILITY

When it came time to take our trip, each of my kids printed off all the info for their portion of the journey and made a daily agenda in their travel journal. I'd give them responsibilities like "holding the tickets" (yes, I printed a backup copy), or being the navigator when I drove. My son was always in charge of getting us through the airports, to rental cars, and train stations. My girls oversaw checking the agenda to let us know where we were going and what we'd be doing.

It might seem like giving your kids these tasks is too time-consuming, but it holds such value, for them and for you. You're building their confidence, teaching them how to notice things around them, pay attention to signs, and orient themselves in unfamiliar surroundings—all important life skills. And as a parent, it gives me confidence to know they can do these things on their own when they get older.

#5. DOCUMENT IT

For each of our trips (we've now been to seven countries and thirty-two states), I've always made my kids write in a travel journal. Each day we collect things to glue in the journal, such as ticket stubs or postcards, and every night we have quiet time where we update the journal with our adventures. My hope is that these journals become treasures they cherish for the rest of their lives.

TIPS FOR TRAVELING ON A BUDGET

#1. SHORT-TERM RENTALS

Airbnb is great for all the obvious reasons, but most important for me is that it's affordable and puts you right in the heart of the culture. You truly feel like a local, and you can save money by cooking at least one meal at home each day. I've found my kids loved having a home-cooked meal on vacation; it especially helps on those tiring days. We rented an apartment in Venice with a view of the Canal, a villa in Tuscany, and an apartment in Rome with a view of the Coliseum. All had three bedrooms and I didn't spend more than $150 a night. I've since rented in London, Scotland, Ireland, Amalfi, and again in Rome and Tuscany.

#2. FLIGHT DEALS

Set up an airfare alert for the cities you'd like to fly into, that way when they go on sale, you'll get an email. I use Airfare Watchdog, but there are several such sites.

#3. BOOK IN ADVANCE

Book as much in advance as possible. I book train tickets, car rentals, and even excursions before we leave for a trip. This helps me budget and pay for items in small amounts over time, rather than being stressed about how much things will cost when I'm on location.

#4. PAY UP!

Reward your kids for trying new food and using the language with locals, for not complaining or talking back, etc. I find praise and bribes go a long way to get kids excited about travel! I pay a daily allowance when we travel. If they've followed "our travel rules" all day, they earn $25. This way they are the ones spending their money for all stuff they want and learning how to pay for things in a foreign country. It empowers them to operate their own budget, and let's be honest, you'd be spending more than that on all the things they want anyway.

#5. BOOKING FLIGHTS

First, *always* travel on airlines that give you miles through your preferred mileage plan. I won't get on a flight unless I'm earning miles! With miles I've paid (twice) for my daughters and I to go to Italy and it's cost a total of $58 (taxes), so being loyal to your mileage plan is key. Second, buy one-way tickets. This is a little tricky, so these tips really help. This is how I've done all my international travel.

- Buy tickets to your destination city in one transaction. Tuesday is the cheapest day to buy flights.
- Then in a separate transaction (could be at a later date, helps spread out the cost), get the one-way tickets back from the last city on your itinerary.
- Clear your search history and cookies if you are doing a lot of searching for the same routes; the algorithms pick up on your route and prices will go up each time you search.
- Note: you'll need to show your return flight confirmations when you check in as it will look like you're leaving the country without a return flight, so be sure to print off paper copies.

The best part about booking this way is that you don't need to return to the arrival city for your departure, so no wasted travel days. It also means you can pick the airline with the best deal for each flight. This is also much cheaper than choosing the "multi-destination" option and booking as one ticket.

Like I did, most people think it's too expensive to travel internationally with your kids, but if I could do it as a single mom, anyone can. If you do a little research and try these tips, you'd be shocked at how easy and affordable it is to make memories around the world that you and your kids will cherish for life.

LESSON #56

DON'T BE *THAT* MOM

Just don't, it's tacky!

Okay Mama, there's a difference between giving ourselves grace, and holding ourselves accountable for bad behavior. After all, if we are to effectively teach our kids what's "acceptable behavior" and what is not, we've gotta hold ourselves to the same standard, am I right?

Here's my little list of the "tacky mom shit" we should avoid.

NO SCREAMING

We don't appreciate it when our kids are screaming and throwing a fit. Same standard applies, only we are grown-ups so . . . no screaming at our kids, especially in public. It's not an effective way to communicate, it won't get you the results you're after, and it's a bad look. Let's use our "communication voice" instead.

DON'T TOLERATE RUDE BEHAVIOR

Teaching our kids how to behave in public is a big part of our responsibility. We want them to know how to treat people respectfully and check them when they're being disrespectful.

Especially to service professionals. I waited tables for fifteen years and hated when kids were rude and disrespectful to me and their parents did nothing about it. Teach them to say "please" and "thank you" and expect good behavior when you're out and about.

DON'T LET THE KIDS CAUSE HAVOC

When you're out and about, at a restaurant, or anywhere, don't let them run amuck. No throwing things, no food fights in restaurants, no hitting people. If they destroy the place, clean it up and make them help if they are old enough to walk. Or better yet, don't let them destroy it in the first place.

NO BAD-MOUTHING DAD

Really watch what you say about the other parent in the presence of your kids. I know it's hard, whether you're married, divorced, or anywhere in between, but it's our job to protect our kids and throwing the other parent under the bus is a passive aggressive way of also putting your child down. Because your child is half of that parent, and they realize this at a young age, so if you dislike their father, they can interpret that as you disliking *them*. None of us are perfect at this, but make a concerted effort, because it can cause true harm to your child, and it can backfire on you.

My mother chronically put my dad down in front of us kids and complained about him incessantly to us directly, from my earliest memories. All this did was make each of us want to side with my father and pushed us away from her. You might think that it's helping the kids "side with you" but it's not; it's more likely pushing them away.

The best advice people gave me after my divorce was to never talk about it, or my ex, in front of my kids. I made that a rule. Even when my girlfriends wanted to talk about it, if my kids were home, we'd go in another room, or I'd put a movie on for them. I didn't ever want them hearing bad things from me. I knew they loved their dad and wanted it to always stay that way, as that is what's best for them. Even though it's been a very difficult situation from day one, I've tried to keep those tensions and frustrations (as best I could) away from them. It hasn't always worked, though. It has been a brutal fourteen years with very little co-parenting or cooperation on his part, so I know they have felt it, even when I've tried to shield them. And that breaks my heart. But I always believed that if I consistently tried to keep them out of it, they would have a happier, more adjusted childhood and feel loved in both our homes.

LESSON #57

MOMMY TIME

How to take care of you.

I remember when I was married, after the twins were born, I couldn't wait until my husband got home because that meant I could go to the grocery store, *alone*. It would be the only moment of alone time I'd get all day, and I can still see myself walking as slowly as possible down each aisle, trying to drag out every quiet moment. That was my "me time," and it wasn't every day, or even every other. There wasn't much awareness back then of how important a little alone time is for a mom, how it helps keep her sane and recharges her batteries.

Work was my alone time after the divorce, it was my chance to be an adult and disconnect temporarily from my mommy role. But once I started working from home, those lines got blurry, and it was much harder to feel like a grown-up when I was home all day talking to just my kids.

It's not always easy to get in some quiet time, but it's so important. It's like anything else, and once you see the value in doing it, you'll find the time. I've used either yoga, the gym, or my Barre3 class, to schedule alone time outside the house each day.

When my kids were small, their early bedtime meant I had a few hours to myself each night.

Establishing boundaries also helped me get a little peace when needed during the day. I love meditation, so if I'm having a rough day or just need some alone time, I've taught my kids that this is "mama's time," and unless the house is burning, there's no disrupting me.

COACHING

Make time alone a priority. It can be just a few minutes of quiet in your room each day, or getting a manicure once a week, or the gym, whatever works for you. This gets easier as your kids get older, especially when they go to school. But even if you're home with your first baby, take time for yourself. It's perhaps most crucial if you're a new mom. You need that time to recharge, to clear your head, to rest, and to feel "normal." Take it with zero guilt! Your baby will be just fine without you for a bit (provided you didn't leave them home alone.).

GIVE YOURSELF GRACE

Don't be so hard on yourself, Mama.

This is a lot, I know. Being responsible for creating, molding, nurturing, and raising human beings is a massive job. It's endless, and sometimes it's suffocating. It is the biggest paradox.

One minute you're sobbing because your nipples are cracked and bleeding, and your sweet baby still hasn't latched properly, and won't stop crying with that accusing tone, because he knows you're intentionally starving him to death. And you feel like the worst mom on earth. Then you're peeing yourself because your eight-month-old has hiccups and can't stop laughing, which got you laughing, and now you're hysterical, and you need to change out of those wet yoga pants and put on clean sweats, but you haven't done laundry in God knows how long, and there are no clean sweats.

One morning you're laughing because your two-year-old just did the most adorable thing a toddler has ever done in the history of humanity, and that afternoon you're fantasizing about putting a pillow over your head and screaming until you black out. One day you're joking effortlessly with your teenager, the next they're slamming doors in your face, rolling their eyes, and back-talking under their breath.

And one day, they pack up their room, and you hide their favorite stuffed animal in their suitcase and drive them to collage. And you can't stop crying because, it's over. It's all over. All those unimaginably hard, endless days, days filled with inexplicable joy and boundless love, are over. And you just can't believe it. It came in like a tornado and now it's eerily calm.

And you sit at home, in the quiet and wonder, *did I do a good job? Are they okay? Was I a good mom?*

And your phone buzzes, and it's your baby boy. He says, "Mama, today in practice, coach asked us all to talk about our 'why.'"

And you respond, "He did? I love that! What is your why?"

And your baby, your sweet toddler, your cranky teen, and now your young man says, "It was you, Ma. My why is you."

You're doing a good job, Mama, even when it doesn't feel like it. Give yourself grace. They will see it all and appreciate it one day. And in a moment that takes your breath away, eighteen years of love, sweat, and tears will all pay off.

PART SIX

ON LIFE . . .

Lessons to help you—*Be the best you and live the best life!*

This section is all about sharing the biggest lessons I've learned about life. They are ones I coach on a regular basis, and things I've used to improve myself and help me build a life I love.

There's a lot here, so as always, take what speaks to you. My hope is that as you go through various stages of life, this book will still be relevant. I've learned in coaching, that something can resonate with you very differently depending on where you're at in life, or on any given day. We receive things differently based on what we need in that moment. So, no worries if some of it isn't for you today, maybe it will be later, maybe not. My goal is to just share what I know in hopes some of it lands with impact, on the day you needed to hear it.

LESSON #59

EMBRACE YOUR STORY

How to value your biggest asset.

Your story is your greatest asset. It's the one thing that is uniquely you. It's something no one can take from you, or replicate. It is your competitive advantage.

When I first started blogging in 2009, I did so anonymously. My blog, *Thoughts.Stories.Life.,* was the one place I could entirely be myself, unfiltered and real. It was the only "person" I had to talk to about all the shit going on in my life. It was how I sorted my thoughts and tried to make sense of past. It's where I was honest about how hard things were, and how much I was struggling to put my life back together. And it's where I started sharing my dreams and my plans for the future. All of that was terrifyingly personal, and I never intended for anyone to discover it was me.

And then one day, on my first business trip to New York City, an article I'd written and submitted (I thought anonymously) to a huge website, was published with my name. It was my whole story, my divorce, the fact that I was really a broke single mom struggling to make ends meet, that I had all these dreams and how some of them were beginning to manifest, all of it. The article went viral almost immediately. I remember sitting in my hotel room with the Google alert, panicking. I felt exposed and terrified of the repercussions. I just knew I'd lose my job.

But I was there to work, so I pulled myself together and went downstairs to meet a favorite client for lunch. For whatever reason (the Universe knew what it was doing), I opened up to Bill. I told him the whole story, sharing my fear that the public knowing my story, would end me.

He looked at me and said, "Sarah, that is your story? I had no idea. That is an incredible story."

"Thanks, but what do I do about it?" I trusted his advice; he is a big-time lawyer after all, so I knew he'd give it to me straight.

"You own it," he said. "You own your story, Sarah. You don't run from it, you embrace it. It's incredible what you've been through and how you're trying to put your life back together and it makes me respect your hustle and character even more. That is your asset, own it."

I've gotten a lot of incredible advice in my life, there's been several times when I've sat across from someone and in the moment, knew I was receiving life-changing advice. But this was by far the number-one piece of wisdom anyone has ever given me. It changed my life. I would not be here today without it.

That advice helped me get comfortable with my story and changed how I viewed it. It was no longer something I was trying to run from or hide, it wasn't this giant embarrassing secret; it was my past and I was intentionally creating a new future in spite of it. I learned how to be proud of that, and not ashamed.

It takes a while to see your own story in this light, but when you do, things can shift in the best possible way. We all have a story. Maybe yours is dramatic like mine, maybe not, it doesn't matter; either way you have a past that has taught you something. What is it? How have you grown or evolved from it?

COACHING

In my life coach training program, I teach new coaches how to identify and share their story, and here are some of those tips.

- What are some of the big highlights of your past?
- Is there adversity you've overcome? If so, what?
- Have you achieved something unique, great, special? How did you do this?
- What are things you've learned from past experience?
- Did something happen to you in the past that you've learned how to move on from? How did you accomplish this?
- What is your "before" and "after"? Looking at your story from this angle may really help you put it together. Or what is your "before," and what is your dream-case "after"? That can help you identify your desired outcomes.
- What part of your story could others relate to or learn from? How can you share your story in a way that others see a reflection of themselves?

Answering these questions will help create a framework for your story. Then, write it as a two-page descriptive essay; this will help you include the details and make it more captivating. Start with the "before" how things used to be, how you used to feel, and then describe how things are now (or how you want them to be). Re-read and re-write this story many times. Leave it for a week or two and re-write it again. Once you've gotten this two-pager tight, meaning it's condensed and powerful and says everything you'd like to convey, then write a paragraph version of it. Do the same thing, condense it down, make it strong.

Read it aloud. Send it to a friend who will provide meaningful feedback and adjust if needed.

And then at some point, you must set it free. Put it out into the world and trust that everything will be okay. It will feel uncomfortable, exposing, raw, formidable, and maybe even embarrassing, but those feelings soon fade. Once you own your story it's only hard to share the first few times you do it in each format. The first time it's out there in print (like a blog or social media post), the first time you speak it out loud (to someone, on a podcast, or in front of an audience), and the first time you see or hear someone else share your story (like a bio or intro synopsis, an interview or article), those are the hardest. But believe me, it gets easier each time. Now I can talk about my story with no emotional attachment whatsoever. I've shared it ad nauseam, so it just rolls off my lips, but that was certainly not the case in the beginning, so give it time.

Whatever your story is, whatever you've overcome, chances are millions of people have been through the same thing and will take comfort, relate, or learn something from your bravery in sharing your truth.

PRO TIP: You can also do this for specific parts of your journey. For example, with my coaches, they start out writing their story as it relates to "before" they learned the HBRMethod™ (the tools I teach) and "after." This helps to identify and convey where they were *before*, how they felt, what they struggled with, what they wanted to change, and then how their lives have changed *after.*

LESSON #60

MINDSET IS EVERYTHING

How to train your brain to get what you want.

We've talked a lot about mindset throughout these lessons because it's a massive part of getting anything you want. Our mind is the body's core operating system, it runs the show, so learning how to control it changes literally everything.

When your mind is not intentionally directed, it wanders. And for most of us, it wanders off in the opposite direction of where we want to go. It is famous for finding rabbit holes to burrow in, worst-case scenario roads to get lost on, negative oceans that pull us under, and countless other ways to distract and impede our success.

Imagine you are standing at a fork in the road, deciding which path to take. To the right is everything you want; it might be a bumpy road, but its destination is exactly where you want to end up. Now, to the left is everything you know you do not want. It is a cul-de-sac leading you in circles, re-creating past bad behaviors dictated by the same old thoughts. As you stand there deciding what to do, the new voice in your head says, *go right.* The *nasty bitch* in your head says, *why bother? Just stay left, it's what we know.*

You decide to go right. *Yay, you!* New outcomes, here we go. But wait. We forgot to relay this new information to our operating system and so our mind went left. Here we are, struggling, and hustling to go right without our operating system. Shit, we never knew this road would be so difficult. *Why is it so hard? Why is nothing I'm trying, working? I really want to turn back and go left, this sucks.* Ever been there? I sure have, and it does suck, a lot.

We can't get very far if our thoughts/mindset (a.k.a. operating system) are not in alignment with where we want to go. It becomes a battle, making every action ten times harder than it needs to be, because we are split, heading in two opposing directions. Our desire and hustle are trying to create new outcomes, but our mind is just rehashing old thoughts that produce the same old outcomes repeatedly, despite our effort.

We need to get our mind to take this new journey with us. And if you don't know how to do that, it can be incredibly frustrating.

HOW TO ALIGN YOUR MINDSET

Here are several simple ways to sync your thoughts/mindset with your desired outcomes, so they are in alignment and heading in the same direction.

1. Begin incessantly telling yourself the outcomes you want. Write it out in a detailed story. This is what I want. Use "I will," "I am," or "I have." Always write your story as a declaration that you've received what is to come, not what you wish (or want) for it, but what will absolutely be. Do this even if you do not believe it yet. Write it as

if it's promised or is your current reality. This *is* what's happening.

2. Use mottos and "I am" statements to continuously reinforce this new story, all day every day. "I am succeeding." "I am capable." "I am making things happen." "I am transforming." "I am wealthy." "I am loved."

3. Silence any internal voices that try to make you relive old outcomes. Notice when they pop up and reverse them. Negative voice: "You will never achieve your goal." Reverse it: "I am achieving my goals." "I am proud of the work I'm putting in." "It's only a matter of time before I see results."

Remember, the things you focus on and think about are what is manifesting in your reality. So, the first step in changing this, is to begin choosing your thoughts wisely by purposefully telling yourself the outcomes you want. Over time, your brain will rewrite its operating system to align with those thoughts, words, and desired outcome. Our minds are so cool! It will do anything we instruct, as long as we stay consistent and diligent with the messaging.

PRO TIP: This works for absolutely everything. It's true in relationships, your career, your self-image, your ability to do or achieve anything, your goals, any belief, and anything you want. And it all works the exact same way. Line up your thoughts with the outcomes you want, stop the alternative voice telling you otherwise, and you'll be on your way to receiving anything you desire. It really is that simple.

JUST BREATHE

Clear the noise and calm your mind.

Before I started my personal development journey, I thought meditation and breathing practices were a bunch of New Age fluff. Something over-paid actors did to seem cool and grounded.

I was so wrong.

Even after I knew I should be meditating, it took me years to give it a serious try. I didn't get the point; *how do you sit in silence? Why would you want to?* I remember watching *Eat Pray Love*, and thinking, *why though? Why would I sit for hours in the heat, letting flies land on me? What's the draw?* I definitely didn't get it. And this made me feel kinda dumb.

But slowly I started listening to short, guided meditations on YouTube, for the specific things I was actively working to improve. Whenever I felt old thoughts and beliefs around money or lack start creeping up, I'd go lay down and listen to a fifteen-minute guided meditation on creating abundance. I began to understand how powerful these were in changing my subconscious belief systems. I was doing everything in my power at a conscious level to change those behaviors, but still subconsciously I knew something was blocking my results.

The more I integrated these short practices into my daily life the more I felt their benefit. I began getting faster results—a surprise check would arrive in the mail, a new client would come out of the blue, abundance began showing up in all kinds of new and exciting ways.

And then one day, maybe a year after I started, I got it. I noticed, for the first time, that when I listened to the words, the act of listening itself cleared all other thoughts from my mind. *Ohhhh, so the point of this thing is to clear your mind, and that's what everyone's been talking about!* It wasn't automatic, sometimes it was only for a split second, a few times it's been for minutes at a time, but now I understand the true genius of meditation. A reprieve from our daily thoughts of stress, negativity, anxiety, or worry, even for a moment at a time, is a true miracle. Those fleeting flashes of a pure mind inspire new ideas, change beliefs, stop negative manifesting, and start positive manifesting. It's incredible.

COACHING

Take time to breathe. Use your breath to calm your nervous system when you feel triggered, stressed, or sense an onslaught of anxiety. Use it to provide a moment of pause before reacting to situations, or before saying something you'll later regret. Take a deep breath. Then take five more. Close your eyes, exhale. Now, can you see things clearer? Can you be more objective? More empathetic? Now can you change that thought instead of letting it suck you in?

When you are nervous, take slow deep breaths.

When you are scared, do the same.

When you need strength, this is how you pull it from your inner self.

When you need patience, breathe.

When you are feeling ungrateful, take ten deep breaths and think of how thankful you are that your lungs are working.

Our breath is nature's miracle tonic. It works for everything. It is life after all.

Give meditation a try if you haven't already. I love the guided meditations on YouTube, because you can search by topic and start like I did, by listening to short ones that relate to whatever you need today.

LESSON #62

ANYTHING IS POSSIBLE

Imagine the impossible.

Daydreaming is not for losers. In fact, it's an important piece to the puzzle of success. Without the ability to fantasize and create alternate realities in our mind, no one would ever live their dreams in real life. It allows you to imagine, with vivid clarity, an outcome that does not currently exist.

When I was a kid, I spent endless hours daydreaming, completely immersed in my various make-believe worlds. I crafted these fantasies like a writer does a novel. Spending hours on a specific moment, or conversation, getting it just right. I could see it all play out as clearly in my mind as if watching on a big screen. I could take an idea and turn it into a dynamic, exciting mental movie, one I'd spend weeks expanding and perfecting.

What I didn't know then that I understand now, is just how important visualization is to creating our desired outcomes. It is a critical element to achieving anything we want. Before we can put a plan in place, or become an expert, or do anything else, we must first see it in our imagination.

Which is why it's so important to allow our mind to imagine the "impossible." If we block our big dreams at this elementary stage, what chance will they have of ever developing into something tangible?

In my book *Hustle Believe Receive*, I shared a story about Kanen and Michael Oher. It is by far the manifesting story that everyone wants to hear me tell again and again, because it demonstrates this point so perfectly. Without re-telling all the details here, I'll just say that when Kanen was seven years old, his dream was to attend a Ravens game in Baltimore and meet Michael Oher, who was the subject of the movie *The Blind Side*. This was the biggest dream either of us could imagine at the time and it felt completely impossible. I had no money, no connections, and no way to make his dream a reality.

But I did have belief in the "impossible." I was already manifesting using my Futureboards™ methods and knew that anything was possible. So together we sent that dream into the Universe.

Less than a year later, we were standing on the sidelines at a Ravens game in Baltimore with Michael Oher posing with my son for a photo. (*You've really gotta read that story in* Hustle Believe Receive, *it's mind-blowing!*) Anyway, the more incredible part is the dream it planted in my son that day.

When Kanen started playing football in fifth grade he was a shy, timid kid. There was nothing aggressive about his nature, which conflicted drastically with his imposing physical size and presence on the field. He was a big kid, so the assumption was, he would dominate. But he really didn't. Football was hard for him, but he genuinely loved it. I started taking him to Oregon Ducks games when he was six years old, and football was our thing. Each time we went to a game, I'd say, "Imagine what that would be like, to run out of the tunnel as a Duck, how cool would that be?"

When he got to high school, his dream got serious. He wrote his goals out every year, focused on his fitness, changed his diet, and got very clear about what he wanted. "I'm gonna get a Division I (DI) scholarship to play football, Mama." He told me at the start of his sophomore year. He'd only played a few games on the Junior Varsity team his freshman year, before breaking his ankle and sitting out the remainder of the season. "Okay," I said. "You've got this!"

He fought relentlessly for a spot on the varsity team sophomore year, never missing a practice, and working hard in the offseason to improve. The hard work paid off and not only did he make the varsity team, he played a lot, until he blew his knee out in the last game of the season.

I remember sitting by his bed while he did his physical therapy exercises, surrounded by all the photos of Oregon football players on his wall. He was devastated; what if he couldn't play again? "You'll come back stronger," I told him. "Keep your focus on what you want, honey. Keep dreaming of the day you get to run back on that field."

Junior year he had a breakout season, and then COVID hit, and his senior season was postponed to right before graduation. He realized that if he wanted to live his dream of becoming a DI football player, he would need to do the recruiting himself. So, he made highlight reels and got meetings with coaches across the country, on his own. He got meetings with some pretty impressive schools, Stanford, Brown, Columbia, Washington, but nothing with Oregon and no offers followed. While schools around the country were back in session and seniors played their final season for scouts, Oregon schools were still closed.

And then in January of 2021, his first DI offer came through, from a small private college in Indiana. My heart broke a little at the thought of him so far away, but I was incredibly proud of him for achieving his dream. In April, his senior season finally began, and he was a beast. He'd spent the previous eighteen months training for that moment and he was ready to shine. In the final game of the season (what in a normal year would have been the state championship game), he showed out in a massive way.

I could feel his disappointment afterward that he'd not been able to play his senior season in the fall, when it could have made a difference with his recruiting. Now it was too late, all the big schools had wrapped up recruiting months ago. He was grateful for the offer he'd received and was making plans to head to Indiana after graduation, but still, I knew he was disappointed.

"Why not try one more time?" I asked. "What could it hurt?" So, he made a new highlight reel which included his final game, the big standout performance, and sent it to Oregon. Two weeks later he was offered the very last spot on the team, as a preferred walk-on at the University of Oregon.

Kanen just finished his red-shirt freshman season as an Oregon Duck. I got to watch my boy run out of the tunnel at Autzen Stadium for every home game. I watched him signal the offensive plays at the Stanford away game and saw him warm up with his teammates at the Alamo Bowl in Texas. It's been the realization of our most "impossible dream."

Oh, and even though he hasn't been awarded an athletic scholarship yet, he's at Oregon on a full academic one. Proving once again, that if you allow yourself to simply imagine the "impossible," you are creating the possibility of living it.

Anything truly is possible.

What is your "impossible" dream?

LESSON #63

LISTEN MORE

Practice the art of hearing people.

Are you a good listener? How do you demonstrate this? Because listening isn't just about hearing someone talk in the moment, it's about processing what they say and using that information to build a better connection. That's the difference between listening (being quiet while someone else talks) and hearing them.

When you really hear someone, you are contemplating what they say, you're trying to receive it the way they intended without adding personal interpretations. When you hear, you try to adapt accordingly based on what they have communicated. If your partner said they love it when you hold their hand in public, for example, if you've truly heard them, you'll reach for their hand as you walk down the street. If you hear when your partner talks, you'll know exactly what to get them for their birthday, or on a Tuesday to make them feel special.

Hearing is about paying attention and digesting the information in a way that makes you a better friend, lover, mom, sister, and person. It's about valuing the person enough to not talk over them. To not speak on their behalf. To not put words in their mouth. And to not jump to conclusions.

This is something I continue to work on every day; it's not something I've ever been naturally good at. It takes work, awareness, and the desire to improve. My kids have been great teachers because they have no problem calling me out if I'm assuming, jumping to conclusions, putting words in their mouth, or not paying attention when they are talking.

Hosting a podcast has also taught me how to become a better listener and helped me see how annoying it is when someone constantly speaks over you, something I used to be very guilty of. I've learned that listening is about patience (something I was not born with either), and the respect to allow the other person to reach their point on their own time.

Like any personal development work, it takes awareness that a behavior needs to change, and requires a concerted effort to continuously make improvements. But it's worth it. I am a much better listener than I was even a few years ago and consistently work hard at it. I believe it's made me a better mom (for sure), friend, coach, and leader.

LESSON #64

HAVE EMPATHY

Put yourself in their shoes.

You don't need to be an empath to exhibit empathy. You don't have to feel what another person is feeling, to imagine yourself in their shoes. To me, empathy is an expression of humanity itself. It's the ability (natural or cultivated) to understand where another person is coming from. You don't need first-hand knowledge of every human experience to feel empathetic, you just need to tap into your humanity.

It always helps me to visualize how it would feel if I swapped lives with that person for a day. What would I do? How would it feel to be faced with their decisions? How would I react to the things they are facing? It helps me see things a little clearer from their perspective.

How can you practice being more empathetic? How can we learn to understand people better from their perspective instead of our own?

One of the biggest ways, I've found, is to reserve judgment or pause advice. Listen first, ask questions, imagine being in their position and seeing things through the lens of their life and experience. Try not to react as *you* for a moment, and instead be on their side. Practice the art of understanding.

LESSON #65

BE KIND

Give a little love.

A little kindness goes a long way. It's amazing what can be accomplished with a smile and a little genuine civility.

I always told my kids when I dropped them off at school, "Make someone's day!" It's been a good reminder for us that sometimes the smallest kindness, or even a smile can make another person's day.

Being kind comes with a built-in reward—it brings joy to both the giver and receiver in a way few other things do. It also multiplies, coming back to us in unexpected ways. Sometimes the difference between being short with someone or being kind, is just a split-second decision. In that moment, ask yourself, how do I prefer to be treated? Take a deep breath, gather yourself, put on a smile, and proceed with kindness.

COACHING

How can you make someone's day today? Can you tell the clerk at the grocery store that she looks beautiful? Can you tell the woman walking towards you on the sidewalk that you love her dress? Can you pick up the tab for the car behind you at the drive-through?

Today's the day, spread a little kindness.

LESSON #66

LESSONS LEARNED

Take responsibility, learn from your mistakes.

In my teens and twenties, I thought I knew it all, yet knew very little. In my thirties, life showed me just how much I still had to learn. In my forties, I became very self-aware, with an intense need to learn from my past, my patterns, and my mistakes, in an effort to evolve and stop sabotaging myself.

It took me a long time to learn how to objectively analyze my behavior, take responsibility for my mistakes, and then make changes. It's about accountability. Being accountable for our actions, accepting the consequences, and moving on in a way that ensures we don't make the same mistake twice.

If someone has called you out on a behavior that has hurt them, or pointed out a character flaw that you need to acknowledge and address, take responsibility. It's a huge growth opportunity. Ask how you could do things differently in the future. Learn how to change the behavior by reading, watching videos, going to therapy, getting a coach, or doing other personal work. Instead of getting defensive or being the victim, take ownership and don't do it again.

COACHING

Look back on your life and trace patterns of behavior. Have you been told more than once by several different people that you come off as _____ (aggressive, for instance)? Instead of being defensive about it, change the behavior so that what you say will be heard rather than dismissed as aggressive.

Just because you've done things one way your whole life, does not mean it's right. It could be harming you and those around you. Is there a better way? Could you show up differently? I hate the, "that's just who I am, deal with it," bullshit excuse. Who you are can and should change as you mature, gain life experience, become more educated, and evolve into a better version of yourself. If you don't know how to make those changes, get expert advice.

The bottom line is, if you are making the same mistake more than twice, the problem is you. That's not a criticism, just the fastest way to analyze and change the piece you control. Ask yourself how you can change, adapt, or do things differently to ensure you learn from your mistakes instead of duplicating them.

LESSON #67

KARMA'S GOT YOU

. . . so take the high road.

Karma is a beautiful thing; give it time to work its magic. I've seen this play out countless times in my life, and I know for certain that if you do the right thing (even when you don't want to) and practice patience, Karma will always have your back. It will deliver the sweetest validation.

So, if you are tempted to get revenge on someone who's wronged you, or are dying to stoop to their level, take a moment and breathe. Just give it time; the high road always pays off in the most delicious and satisfying ways.

LESSON #68

FIND JOY

Make yourself happy.

When I wrote *Hustle Believe Receive*, I featured over fifty stories of people who were living their dreams, and I'll never forget my interview with NFL veteran running back Jonathan Stewart. I asked him what his dream was, and his answer shocked me. "To have joy. Joy is what guides me."

It blew my mind. *Joy? Who has joy?* I thought.

That has stuck with me, and became a personal mission. I wanted to find joy. I needed to understand what it meant to feel joyful. It seemed like such an angelic aspiration, one mere mortals couldn't dream of achieving, but if Jonathan felt joy, I wanted to get some too.

"Happiness is fleeting, but joy lasts forever," he told me.

I've spent the past several years uncovering what brings me joy, and I think I understand now what he meant. Joy is a state of being; it is a choice. Happiness is often something we wait for, or expect to receive from an outside source, it's temporary, it feels situational and out of our control. But joy is a conscious decision, one you commit to daily.

Now I understand the vital role joy plays in our over-all wellbeing and how critical it is to living a balanced, happy life. Understanding what brings you joy becomes a powerful tool, one you can use any time to de-stress, relieve anxiety, feel grounded and grateful, and reset your mental state.

COACHING

What makes you happy? What do you enjoy doing? What did you used to love doing as a kid or teenager? What did you make time for before you had a job, kids, husband, etc.? What activity helps take your mind off everything else?

It takes a while for most women to find their "passions and joys," so be patient with yourself, these aren't things we used to value, but we will moving forward. Approach it the same way we made our kids try new things: take a class, sign up for some lessons, give it time. Don't quit after the first class; give it several, and you'll discover that it might grow on you over time. Passions take time and attention to stick, and the more you make them a valued part of your life, the richer their benefits will be.

Here's a few examples of mine to help you understand what types of things can be "passions and joys." Mine are photography, reading novels (or listening to them), gardening, cooking, travel of course, learning Italian, riding horses, wine. Interestingly, all but two of those are things I loved doing as a girl. So, take a moment to examine who you were at ten or fourteen, and there will likely be clues into what brings you joy.

LESSON #69

IF IT DOESN'T SERVE YOU . . .

It doesn't serve anyone.

This lesson might rattle a few cages because it goes against everything we've been taught. We've been told: *Serve. Serve. And serve some more.* I hear it ad nauseam from social influencers, *you've gotta serve your audience. Serve the people. Give everyone what they want. Bleed yourself to death serving everyone but yourself. Be of service!*

I can't.

Here's what I think. If it doesn't serve *you*, it doesn't serve anyone.

I'll tell you what happens when you *serve, serve, serve,* and are trying your best to be a selfless saint about it . . . you get pissed off. You become a martyr. As much as we want this service to come from a pure, kind, loving, and generous place, eventually it backfires, if it's not also serving you.

Here's my question. As women we've realized this to be true when it comes to our traditional roles as wife and mother. We've learned in the past decade or so all about self-care, about "me time," and we now understand these are not "selfish" things. So,

256

why is the opposite message being shoved down our throats from social influencers about everything else? If you want to build a business, they say, *be of service, serve, serve, serve.*

I'm sorry, but if I want a business, *why am I giving everything away, feeling taken advantage of, and not making money?* It doesn't make sense, unless your only goal is to be social media famous, then yes, you must give the people what they want, continuously. Your audience owns you.

Don't get me wrong, I love Instagram (most of the time), and I love the people who engage with me on social media, but I do what works for me. That being said, I'm sure my audience would be three times the size if I could just *serve serve serve.* But I can't. It's not good for me. It's not healthy. It makes me angry, because I'm not a fan of working ten times as hard for half as much. It's not a good feeling.

A few years ago, I almost deleted all my social media. I just couldn't do it anymore. I'd been giving and giving for over a decade. Exposing my life, providing free coaching, sharing my ups and downs, since 2009. I was exhausted, and it was not paying my bills. It was not making me Instafamous. It was not giving back. I was over it.

So, I stepped away for a few weeks to reassess, and asked myself, *what serves me?* It felt like a horrific question to ask. I was a horrible person, how dare I admit, even to myself, that I too needed something from this arrangement. It had to start giving something to me in return, otherwise it was not worth the frustration.

This was a radical, scary idea.

I thought about it for a while. Then I wrote down what served *me.* What did I enjoy about sharing myself, my life, and my knowledge with the world? What did I enjoy about social media? What did I hate about it? What triggered me to feel frustrated, angry, unseen, unheard, used, or unappreciated? I wrote down everything I'd been keeping in my near-exploding brain. This list became my social media boundaries.

Once I knew my triggers, knew what served me, and what didn't, then I could make some important decisions.

1. I detoxed from my phone (Lesson #73)
2. I either muted or unfollowed influencers in my field (who were not personal friends), because I realized seeing how "perfectly" everyone else was showing up to serve all day, was not helping.
3. I unfollowed pretty much everyone else who was not a personal friend, because I didn't want Instagram to be the massive time-suck it had been for years. With less of a feed to follow I could be on and off in seconds, instead of thirty minutes.
4. I followed a few accounts (three or four) of things that bring me joy. Now, instead of my feed causing me to feel triggered or "less than," it makes me smile. I followed Highland coos (look them up, basically the most adorable creatures alive!). And an Italy photography profile, and one from each country we've visited, so I could randomly see a place we'd been pop up in my feed. This always makes me smile and brings back amazing memories.
5. I outlined the activities I *enjoy doing* on social media, to share my knowledge, but don't make me feel all those negative emotions. And I just do those. I know I'm not doing social "right" anymore; my audience should be growing like everyone else's, but I'm doing it right for me. It works for me, and hopefully brings value to those who follow my journey. I've learned that it's okay to do your own thing.

COACHING

If doing what everyone says to do is making you miserable, then stop. Take inventory, find what's wrong, write it down. Write a list of what serves you and what doesn't, then implement new rules and stick to them.

I am soooooo much happier now. I don't let social media control me the way it used to. Now it feels like a blessing, a way to connect that feels good and positive.

> **PRO TIP:** This concept should apply to just about everything in your life. Ask yourself, *what works for me?* Don't just do what other people tell you to, or want you to do, but stop and ask yourself that question. There is nothing selfish about it. You are always an equally valued part of any equation, so if you're only thinking about other people, that takes you out of the equation, which is not cool. You should have a say, a voice in everything. And it's perfectly acceptable to say, *you know what? That actually does not work for me, but here's what does.*

LESSON #70

KEEP YOUR WORD

To yourself and others.

I've talked a lot about keeping our word to ourselves in these lessons, because it's so important. But it's equally important to keep your word to others. If you say you are going to do something, do it. If you don't think you can, don't say you will.

It's simple. Your word matters, and if no one can trust it, that means they can't trust you. The follow-through is everything. We hate it when someone promises something but doesn't deliver, so don't be a hypocrite.

LESSON #71

PAY YOUR OWN WAY

Don't be a mooch.

No one likes a freeloader, so unless you're on a date, pay your own way. Don't let the other person (friend, family member, whoever) pick up the tab all the time. You should always offer to split the bill, and if they paid the last time, it's your turn.

This might seem like basic common sense, but you'd be shocked how quickly people become freeloaders when one person has a higher (perceived or otherwise) net worth than the other. The assumption quickly becomes, the one with the most money should pay, but that's a quick way to get blacklisted from your circle of influence, or just piss-off your friends.

Also, don't expect free shit. As someone whose business is a service, I can't tell you how many times people have expected a "hookup" on my coaching, or an event ticket, because they know me. I've seen this with my entrepreneur friends as well, people in their circle asking for (or expecting) either a steep discount or a freebie. If you're a good friend, you will want to support your friend's business, not take advantage of it.

That said, there's nothing wrong with trading services if it's a win for you both. When I first started out, I used to trade coaching for personal training, for Reiki sessions, for massages. But only when it was an equal exchange of services, and only when both parties needed and wanted the other's service.

LESSON #72

DON'T BE LATE

It's rude.

Here's the thing about being late—it's disrespectful. Now, this is coming from someone who's *not* obsessed with being early, I'm not one of those people who show up thirty minutes before meetings begin, or arrive at parties when the host is jumping out of the shower. I'm never more than a few minutes early to anything. But I am dedicated to being on time. I hate being late, partly because it is a negative single-mom stereotype that annoys the hell out of me (apparently, we are all a hot-mess train-wreck if TV and movies are to be believed), but mostly because I think it's rude.

I absolutely hate when people waste my time, flake, don't show up, or are late to meetings when I've made an effort to show up on time. It's a serious pet peeve and something I have clear boundaries around. If someone is late once, totally understandable, we've all been there a million times. But twice, that is an issue. Three times and I'm done. Why? Because that speaks to the person's character, it's either someone who doesn't plan their time well, or someone so self-focused that they don't even see the problem; either way, I don't have time for it.

Be respectful and be on time. Whether it's meeting a girl-friend for drinks or a business meeting, same rules apply.

LESSON #73

GET OFF YOUR PHONE!

And pay attention.

Do you understand how insanely rude it is to be on your phone when someone is trying to talk to you? I have no idea how humans have gotten away with this behavior for the past few decades, but it's gotta stop.

I can't stand it when I'm talking to someone who thinks everything on their phone is more important than the person standing in front of them. It is such dismissive behavior. It's hard to feel heard, valued, interesting, or important when the person you're speaking to would rather be on their phone.

Three years ago, I began detoxing from my phone because I could see what a nasty habit it was, and because I was trying to teach my teenagers not to be rude. It was hard at first, I'm not gonna pretend it wasn't, but like anything else, if you are committed it gets easier quickly.

To help me reduce my addiction I did these three things:

1. I turned off all notifications from social media. Yes, turned them off *completely*. This means I am not owned and oper-

ated by my Instagram account. There are no little blue "unread" dots calling my name all day long. I open the app when I feel like it, which is about 200 times less a day.

2. I turned my phone on silent and have never turned the ringer back on.

3. I use the "do not disturb" feature on iPhone 24 hours a day, 7 days a week. It allows me to select my kids and anyone else I choose, as the only ones whose notifications or calls I'll receive immediately.

Girl, this changed my freakin' life! I know it sounds extreme and impossible, and I can hear you saying there is no way you could do it, but you could. It has never kept me from getting a business deal, it's never caused my life to implode. Instead, I control it, and it no longer controls me. I check my work email about once an hour during the business day if I'm not at my desk, but don't check it at night or on weekends (boundaries, ladies). I check to see if there are texts or other messages periodically throughout the day, but I no longer spend my days glued to my phone. If I know I'm expecting a call, then I'll turn on the vibrate feature to make sure I don't miss it, but other than that, there is peace and quiet in my life.

LESSON #74

NOTHING TO PROVE

Except to yourself.
"Your hate is what gave me the strength." —Eminem

Good God, this is a lesson I wish I'd learned in my twenties or thirties. I spent so many years trying to prove, to random-ass people, that I could do "it." Whatever "it" was. I've always felt like people underestimate me, or quickly attempt to put me in various boxes, but I'm an anomaly, baby! I've never fit into one box, or a dozen boxes, and I think that's true of most women. We are layered and interesting, complicated, and fascinating. But why do we feel the need to prove it?

I used to bleed energy on people with names I've long forgotten, who doubted me. Who rolled their eyes when I talked about my dreams, or who outright laughed in my face. I'd try everything to convince them, but it just made me pathetic in their eyes.

That all changed when I learned how to turn "hate" into fuel and started proving to *myself* that I could do it. When it comes right down to it, I was the one who needed convincing, that's why I tried so hard to get others' validation, approval, and belief. Because I didn't believe it myself.

I turned *let me convince you*, into a silent, *just wait, I'll show you*. I no longer needed to advertise my goals, plans, or dreams, I just needed to let the results speak for themselves. Success is the best revenge. If someone is giving you shade, there is no better silencer than doing the thing they said you couldn't.

Proving to myself, my worth, my value, my abilities, desire, dedication, and strength became my silent mission. I wanted to *know*, that I could do anything I set my mind to, regardless of who believed in me. I wanted to prove my haters wrong. And girl, it is the best motivation! It fuels you in the beginning to sting like a bee, silent and effective. To let your actions do the talking and your success be undeniable. But soon, you stop caring what they think, because you are focused on proving yourself right.

I can't tell you how many of my early haters have reached out to say shit like, "Congratulations on your success, I always knew you could do it." *Bitch, please! You did not.*

They may not have known, but I did, and that is all that matters.

So, if you know you are meant for big things, you see a future that no one else sees, that's okay. Every visionary or person you admire, was there once too. We've all been the only one to get our vision, see our potential, or believe in our dreams, and that's normal. They are *our* dreams after all; support is not a prerequisite to our success.

CONTROL WHAT'S WITHIN YOUR POWER

. . .And let the rest go.

One very important lesson I have learned over the years is that stress and anxiety mount when you focus on the things you cannot control. So, when things happen, when life throws me a curveball, or when I'm in a situation that triggers anxiety or stress, I always ask myself this question: What do I control?

I believe we have much more control over our lives, thoughts, outcomes, and situations than we can begin to comprehend. No matter what life throws your way, or how out of control things may feel, we always have a choice. We can focus on what's going wrong (the negative), which is everything we do not control, thereby making it worse. Or we can decide to focus on the possibility that things could somehow turn around and end up in our favor (the positive). The latter is always within our control. So, no matter what, you'll always have that.

But in most situations, there are several components within our control. Our job is to quickly assess and identify what they are. Because the longer we focus on things outside our control, the bigger and more unsurmountable they appear and the more problematic they become, so it's imperative to quickly stop the bleeding.

COACHING

We gain control using these three easy steps:

1. **Identify problem.** What's causing you stress and bringing on anxious thoughts? What are you dealing with? What feels out of control? This step is basically assessing the situation, getting a read on what's happening and how it's making us feel.

2. **Ask yourself: What about this can I control?** This is why we identified the problem first, so we could see the pieces that are outside our control. But if we give it a minute, we'll start thinking of things we can control. Brainstorm here, quickly make note of everything that comes to mind, get a pen, and write a list. Think of *everything.* We know that we always control what we focus on, so that's one. Write down the best possible outcome to your situation; if everything went unexpectedly perfect, what would happen? Now you've identified an outcome you want, and something positive to focus on and put into the Universe. What else do you control? What pieces could you start working to "fix"? Here's where you engage everything you've ever learned about problem-solving, because that's exactly what you're doing. You are looking for unseen solutions, ways you can influence an outcome in your favor.

3. **Start executing your action items.** The faster you begin working on the pieces you've identified as being in your control, the quicker momentum can shift suddenly in your favor. Your focus is soon absorbed with taking

the actions you control, and without even realizing it, the magical element of this sequence kicks in . . . you begin to let go of everything outside your control. When this happens, stress and anxiety fade and are replaced with thoughts and actions pointed in the direction of your desired outcome, thereby creating them.

When you use this three-step process, it can immediately calm anxiety and shift how you feel, both physically and mentally. This alone gives you power and control you would have otherwise not engaged. The more you do this, the quicker long-term results will follow. Remember that the work you do today to gain control also has a delayed reaction, meaning you will see the benefits of your action and focus down the road.

YOUR LIFE CAN CHANGE IN A DAY

For the better.

We often hear people say, with sadness and regret, "Your life can change in a day." But what most don't realize is that it can also change *for the better* in a single day.

I have so many examples of this, but one that stands out is February 14, 2018. It was a year, almost to the day, since I'd left corporate to follow my dream of coaching and speaking full-time, and it was not going well.

A few months prior, I had been begging the Universe for a sign, *any sign*, an indication that I'd made the right decision. "Why is nothing I try working?" I beat my fists and stomped my feet in frustration. "This isn't fair!" A few days pass like this, me feeling sorry for myself, cursing the Universe for giving me a dream I couldn't get off the ground.

Then one morning I woke to an email from a podcaster asking for an interview. *What good will another podcast interview do?* I sulked, and promptly hit delete. I'd been a guest on many podcasts by this point, and none had ever moved the needle in my business, expanded my audience, or seemed to even be a good use of my time. I was burned out and sour.

A week passes as I continue to pout and contemplate giving up. I knew each day that passed was a conscious choice to dig my hole a little deeper, but I didn't care. Ever been there? You know what to do, you get why you should, but you just can't. And of course, as always happens, things began to look darker and bleaker with each passing day.

As I'm standing in my living room, cursing my life, the phone in my palm buzzes with another email from the same podcaster. "I've been reading your book, *Hustle Believe Receive*," he says, "and I can't put it down. I'd really love to have you on my show." I paused. Read it again. *Wait, did he say he was actually reading my book?* That was new, as hosts never read my book, just acted like they did. He listed a few famous names of previous guests and asked if I'd share my 8-step HBRMethod™ on the show.

He had my attention.

So, I did what any breathing human would do. I pulled up his Instagram @edmylett. I clicked on his most recent video post, where he talked about how our life can change for the better in a day. I felt it, my intuition screaming, *this is the message you needed to hear today, girl. You better listen!*

I hit reply to the email and said I'd be happy to come on the show.

Thirty seconds later I get a response, "Can I give you a quick call right now? I have about seven minutes before my next meeting, but I'd love to connect and confirm if you're available."

Who the hell was this guy?!

My phone rings, and I took a seven-minute call that changed my life.

The day our podcast episode aired on his #1 iTunes-rated, *The Ed Mylett Show,* was Valentine's Day 2018. In one day I booked more speaking gigs then I'd done the entire year, my book hit the top 100 which led to a paperback release, a collaboration with Ed, and a lasting friendship.

Your tsunami of good fortune could be just around the corner. It might be one email away, one phone call away, one single day that swings the pendulum in your favor. Wake up every morning and ask yourself, will this be the day when my dreams come true? Will today bring the opportunities I've been hustling for, or the love I've been dreaming of?

Expect good things, and life will surprise you in glorious, unexpected ways.

LESSON #77

GROW YOUR BRAIN

Easy ways to continuously learn and grow.

One of the five core areas of life that I coach clients to focus on is Mind & Body. Under the "mind" category we identify two equal parts, 1). How to clear your mind 2). How to grow your mind. I think both are equally important.

You can't live a healthy or balanced life if you don't know how to de-stress or clear your head, you just can't. That's why I shared lesson #61 on meditation, because that's one of the tools I've used to effectively clear my head and reduce stress. If meditation's not your jam, no problem, but find something that is.

On the flip side, to elevate your life and evolve in any capacity you need to grow your brain. How do you gather knowledge, learn new things, and push yourself intellectually? There's countless ways, so it's important that you find ones that keep you interested, engaged, and change as you grow.

Here are a few ways I focus on growth and push myself mentally.

Reading. I know that not everyone enjoys reading, but it's something you get better at over time and it improves your focus, concentration, vocabulary, knowledge, and brainpower.

Audiobooks. If sitting down to read a book is not your jam, listen to audiobooks. You get the same benefits, especially if they are narrative books such as novels or memoirs. It requires a lot of focus to listen to a story; if you check out for even a minute you could miss a plot twist or an important story development.

I started listening to novels on Audible about two years ago, and now average about 100 books a year. It's dramatically improved my writing, knowledge, and especially my focus. It works like a meditation or an escape, completely clearing my mind of everything else. I'm obsessed. Check out my Amazon page if you'd like some recommendations of books with strong female characters set in international settings, or historical fiction, my favorite genre.

Podcasts. There are a million things you can learn from a million podcasts, just be careful that it's helpful and not just adding "noise" to your day. Try to digest and implement what you're hearing when appropriate; that's the best way to turn knowledge into personal change.

Language Learning. This is a very useful way to challenge your brain and continue to push yourself. I'm learning Italian and have found many ways to incorporate that learning into my daily life. I use a language learning app (I like Drops or Pimsleur), to get in ten to twenty minutes of easy, fun learning on my phone. I've also taken private lessons; iTalki is a great place to find an inexpensive tutor. I put the Italian subtitles on American TV shows, so I can practice reading those translations.

I also watch a lot of Italian shows (there are many great ones on Netflix). And lastly, I use it often. Whatever words I'm learning, I try to incorporate at home with my kids. The line in the dedication to this book is something I say to each of my children every single night, which means "goodnight my love."

Learn a New Skill. What have you always wanted to try? Ice skating? Golf? Cooking? Dancing? Woodworking? Quilting? Horseback riding? Whatever your interests are, learning something new has so many positive benefits, including growing your brain.

LESSON #78

ENGAGE THE EXPERTS

When and how to get outside advice.

I wish I knew long ago how much benefit there is to hiring experts. It is the fastest track to success at anything you want. Growing up poor and having never seen anyone who hired trainers, chefs, tutors, coaches, or any other type of expert, it just wasn't something I thought a normal person could do. It seemed like an elitist thing. Until I got sick of doing everything the hardest way possible and started investing in getting the expertise I needed.

And now, as a master coach, I get it. I see the results clients get after just a few sessions of one-on-one work with me, versus someone who's trying hard to teach themselves the same things. It's night and day. The same has been true every time I've worked with a coach, wether it's in business, personal training, nutrition, or any of the various other experts I've been fortunate enough to work with. All of whom have been well worth the investment.

Working with an expert, whether privately or in a group setting, absolutely fast tracks your results. It's the only way for you to receive customized advice, which is the component that changes everything.

If you have goals, but aren't sure how to achieve them, and you can afford to engage an expert, do it. Every time. It's worth it.

LESSON #79

RAISE THE BAR

Expect more.

What do you deserve? What does your future hold? What do you want it to hold? As you contemplate these questions, I want you to ask yourself: *How can I raise the bar? How can I expect more, aim higher, and stop settling for less?*

I think we women settle for less way too often. And we only do that when our bar is set too low. So, raise that bar, girl! No more accepting unacceptable behavior. No more tolerating disrespect and mistreatment. No more putting ourselves down. No more letting others decide what's best for us, speak for us, or make our decisions. No more telling ourselves we can't do it or that we don't deserve it. No more.

We are powerful, incredible specimens. We respect ourselves and expect the same in return. We are an example to our children, the people in our lives, and ourselves, of what a strong, brave, smart, incredible woman is capable of.

We are fierce chicks, hear us roar! We will settle no more.

LESSON #80

PASS IT ON

Share what you know.

So, these are my top 80 life lessons. Believe it or not, I had to narrow them down from more than a hundred. I hope you have found them valuable and learned helpful tools along the way. Life is an incredible teacher if we pay attention and learn from its lessons. I plan to continue to grow and evolve until my last breath, drinking every ounce of its wisdom. I want to be a student of all life has to teach, and then I want to continue passing on those lessons.

And girl, you have insight too, lessons and wisdom you've learned and can share with the world. What has life taught you? What are some of the things you wish someone had explained, or warned you about ten or twenty years ago? What advice can you pass on to your children, mentees, nieces or nephews, a friend, or the world at large? I bet you know so much more than you give yourself credit for. Start sharing that knowledge.

It has been through coaching that I have learned so much about myself; it's helped hold me accountable. It's through sharing knowledge that I've expanded my own expertise. It's through teaching that I continue to grow. You may think that no one wants your advice, but I promise, someone will.

About ten years ago, I knew a guy who used to regularly scoff at my dream to write a book. It was long before I wrote my first one, but by that time I had attempted several unsuccessfully. "You think you can write actual books?" he poked. "Who's gonna read what you have to say or take your advice? Don't you have to 'be somebody' for that to happen?"

Well, to that douche, and any who might have similar thoughts about your dreams . . . let's show them what a fierce chick can do!

Tag me on Twitter and Instagram @sarahcentrella sharing your biggest life lessons, or your takeaways from mine. I would love to hear them! As Maya Angelou said, "When you learn, teach!"

ACKNOWLEDGMENTS

I would like to take a moment to thank the amazing women in my life who've inspired, influenced, and encouraged me the past several years. Through them, I've learned the true value and joy of surrounding yourself with boss ass chicks!

Thank you to my incredible agent Beth Davey, without her I would not be a published author. She believed in me from the start and has busted her butt on my behalf. You're the best, Beth. Thank you to my amazing editor, Julie Ganz, who took a risk on an unknown writer and published my first book, *Hustle Believe Receive*, and this masterpiece as well! I wouldn't be here without you.

Big appreciation goes to my circle of influence, the women who've inspired me to keep showing authenticity and honesty in this crazy social media-fueled world, your support means the world, ladies: Sheri Salata, Lori Harder, Diann Valentine, Kimberley Hatchett, Jo Frost, Kathy McKabe, LeShonda Martin, Ali Levine, Jessie Lee, Danette May, Telli Swift, Dr. Viviana Coles, and many other female leaders who've shown love and support.

Thank you to the women of my Coaching Circle, you inspire me every single week! Big love to my personal circle, Courtney, Jackie, Mandana, Elisha, Maria, love you bitches!

And lastly, my babies, everything I do, I do for you.

xo

Sarah